THE MEANING
OF
MOBY DICK

THE MEANING OF
MOBY DICK

BY

WILLIAM S. GLEIM

New York

RUSSELL & RUSSELL

IN TOKEN OF MY GRATITUDE

FOR HIS ENCOURAGEMENT

THIS BOOK IS INSCRIBED

TO

A. Edward Newton, LL.D.

THE MEANING OF *MOBY DICK*

HERMAN MELVILLE'S *Moby Dick* is probably the most remarkable mystery story ever written, for the mystery which is hidden in that book has remained unsolved for more than eighty years.

Possibly one reason for the failure to discover the hidden meaning is because readers do not, generally, follow Thoreau's rule, to wit:—"Books must be read as deliberately and reservedly as they were written."*

A good example of the results of unobservant reading may be found in the following lines, taken from an extravagant fantasy, written by a famous poet:—"And Moby Dick will give a great bellow like a fog-horn blowing, and stretch 'fin out' for the sun away in the west."

A careful reader of *Moby Dick* would have discovered that "the whale has no voice." This fact is repeated in the lines:—"the fear of this vast dumb brute of the sea was chained up and enchanted in him; he had no voice." Furthermore, Melville stated that "The great genius of the whale . . . is declared in his pyramidical silence."

NOTE:—All quotations for which no credit is given are taken from the text of *Moby Dick*.

* Walden, Henry D. Thoreau.

[1]

The careful reader would have learned also, that when a whale has stretched "fin out," he is *dead*. This fact is presented in one of the most impassioned outbursts in the book:—"And this is what ye have shipped for men! to chase that white whale on both sides of land, and over all sides of earth, 'till he spouts black blood and rolls fin out." If the phrase "stretch fin out" is intended to mean *to swim*, it is misleading, because "to the whale, his tail is the sole means of propulsion. . . . His side fins only serve to steer by."

Moby Dick is really two stories; an ostensible story that treats of material things; and another story, hidden in parables, allegories, and symbolism, which treats of abstract things. And these two stories are parallel and analogous to each other.

The superficial narrative describes a hunt for a white whale; but the story which it hides tells of a supernatural adventure to carry out the most original and daring scheme for setting this world right that has ever been invented. But aside from the main parable, which shows the ulterior relation between Ahab and the Whale, the other hidden meanings are without sequence, continuity, or coordination. However, they do possess a degree of uniformity, inasmuch as they all relate to the mystery of life and destiny.

The hidden matter also includes analogous allusions to probably all the religions, philosophies, and mysticism of which Melville had knowledge, as well as a few cynical shots, from ambush, at orthodoxy. Indeed, without casting the least doubt upon Melville's sincerity, the book may be regarded as a gigantic hoax, in which he satirized all man-made religions, and challenged the perspicacity of his contemporaries.

Symbolism is as old, or older, than literature, and all writers who mean more than they say, and who also in order to make their meanings more impressive, have made use of symbolism in their works. The power of symbolism is clearly set forth, by Carlyle, as follows:—

"In a symbol there is concealment and yet revelation, here, therefore, by silence and by speech acting together, comes a double significance, and if both the speech be itself high, and the silence fit and noble, how impressive will their union be."*

Therefore, symbols are more effective than similes or metaphors, because a symbol, when properly used, should not have its meaning explained; its meaning should be left for the reader to discover.

However, in order that the reader may be justified in looking for symbols, many works, containing symbolism, maintain a relation between the symbols that are named and explained, and the symbols which may be described as silent, or hidden; and furthermore, it may be assumed, that

* Sartor Resartus.

[3]

when an author calls the attention of the reader to the symbolical significance of certain material things in his story, it serves notice to the reader that the symbolical significance of other material things, which are not explained, may be found in that same story, if the reader will take the trouble to look for it.

There are at least two modern books that include the same mystical theory which furnished the motive in *Moby Dick;* and that theory is; that the abstract correspondence of a material symbol may be affected by the vicissitudes of its material symbol.

One story is *The Scarlet Letter,* by Nathaniel Hawthorne, which was published one year prior to *Moby Dick.* That story is packed with symbolism, and although many of the symbols are clearly explained, fully as many are silent. The silent symbols may be usually found in the descriptions of the settings for the various scenes, which they intensify by providing an appropriate atmosphere.

The incident which is intended to show the mystical power of a symbol, occurred in the forest, during the meeting of Hester Prynne with the Rev. Arthur Dimmesdale.

Hester Prynne, who had worn the scarlet letter, —symbol of her shame, continuously, for seven years, proposed to the minister that they both leave New England, and begin life anew in another country. Dimmesdale agreed, saying:—

" 'This is already the better life! Why did we not find it sooner?'

" 'Let us not look back,' answered Hester Prynne. 'The past is gone! Wherefore should we linger upon it now?

" 'See! With this symbol, I undo it all, and make it as it had never been!'

"So speaking, she undid the clasp that fastened the scarlet letter, and, taking it from her bosom, threw it to a distance among the withered leaves. . . . The stigma gone, Hester heaved a long, deep sigh, in which the burden of shame and anguish departed from her spirit."

It should be noted that the scarlet letter fell "among the withered leaves," for, as withered leaves are a symbol of death, the silent use of that symbol intensifies the meaning of her action, which clearly is, that she consigned her shame to the dead past, or, in other words;—the past is dead, and she is free from its influence.

The other symbolical story, of comparatively recent date, is *The Song of Songs*, by Hermann Suderman. The theme of this story is the mystical correspondence which a musical score, based upon the ancient Hebrew love songs, in the Bible, maintained with the moral life of a young girl, named Lilly Czepanek.

The musical score was completely identified with the personality of the girl, and throughout her life, it reflected in its physical condition, her spiritual or moral status.

At intervals, the mystic influence of the musical score is noted in the story, as when she told her tale to Konrad:—"Told . . . how it had completely filled her girlhood years; though later it had acquired a far loftier and more mysterious significance, becoming a symbol of her deeds."

At a later period, when she endeavored to redeem herself through honorable love, but was cruelly frustrated, she decided to end her life. While making preparations for suicide;—

"She came by chance upon the old score of the Song of Songs. . . . Did it not seem as if this Song of Songs, which lay there debased, stained, decayed, like her own life, had in truth hovered over her, blessing her and granting her absolution from her sins? . . . 'Yes, you shall come along,' she said. 'You shall die when I die.'

"She carefully rolled and wrapped the crumbling sheets. She then set out for the bridge over the river.

"Now her fingers grasped the iron top of the railing.

"All she could see of the water below, was a dark, slimy shimmer. Not even the lamps reflected in it.

"Now, one leap—and the thing was done.

[6]

" 'Yes I'll do it, I'll do it,' a voice within her called.

"But she had to send the Song of Songs ahead. It would be a hindrance to her as she climbed over.

"She threw it—a bit of white flitted by—a splash below—sharp and distinct, which made her tingle all over like a slap in the face. . . .

"When she heard the sound, she knew she would never do it. . . . She sent one more searching look at the lazy waters, in which the Song of Songs had just disappeared.

"Then she turned and went back."

The master-stroke which is hidden in the climax of this story, is in leaving the reader to discover for himself, that when Lilly cast the symbol of her shameful life into the stream of oblivion, which did not even reflect the lamplight, she was entirely parted from her past.

Thus did both Hester Prynne and Lilly Czepanek benefit by the same mystical process; but while Hawthorne makes the meaning of his incident perfectly clear, Suderman, with artful subtlety, leaves his meaning to be discovered by the reader.

In like manner, Melville, in his hidden story, proposed to annihilate a spiritual principal, by destroying its material symbol.

II

THE manner in which the ulterior meanings in *Moby Dick* are hidden, is somewhat similar to the way in which, according to Emanuel Swedenborg, "The Prince of Fantasy," as Hawthorne called him, believed the truths of the Bible are hidden. That is, Swedenborg believed that the Bible was written in symbols, and he interpreted them according to his *Doctrine of Correspondences*.

This doctrine teaches that all material things are symbols of spiritual things, and, therefore, all natural objects mentioned in the Bible, stand for their spiritual correspondences. Swedenborg revealed the "internal sense" of several books of the Bible, which compose the material of his work, entitled, *Heavenly Arcana*.

The difference between the work of Swedenborg, and the work of Melville, is, that whereas Swedenborg *uncovered* Biblical truths; which he believed were hidden in parables and symbols; Melville, in *Moby Dick*, reversed the process, and, by means of parables and symbols, *concealed* allusions to Biblical teachings.

These parables are not merely incidental, as literary embellishments, in *Moby Dick*, for they constitute, rather, the main purpose for which the book was written. The whaling voyage is merely the carrier of a hidden collection of mystical topics.

The relative importance of the material subject and the supernatural subject, is shown in the following paragraph, wherein Melville, after an exhaustive description of everything pertaining to the *material whale*, deftly turned his description to the immeasurable significance of the *symbolical whale*.

"Give me a condor's quill! Give me Vesuvius' crater for an inkstand! Friends, hold my arms! For in the mere act of penning my thoughts of this Leviathan, they weary me, and make faint with their outreaching comprehensiveness of sweep, as if to include the whole circle of sciences, and all the generations of whales, and men, and mastodons, past, present, and to come, with all the revolving panoramas of empire on earth, and throughout the whole universe. Such, and so magnifying, is the virtue of a large and liberal theme. We expand to its bulk. To produce a mighty book, you must choose a mighty theme."

Hyperbolic license would hardly justify the foregoing exaggeration, if it were limited to the material whale, and, in confirmation of the assumption that the lines hold a mystical meaning, we have another paragraph.

"Small erections may be finished by their first architects; grand ones, true ones, ever leave the copestone to posterity. Heaven keep me from ever completing anything. This whole book is but draught—nay but the draught of a draught."

The last paragraph is characteristic of the method employed by Melville, in writing the book. That method was to take advantage of the natural tendency of the reader to keep his attention focused upon the superficial story, and who takes for granted, without stopping to question the obscure passages which surreptitiously expose, for an instant, the deeper meaning of the book.

This same limitation of perception is noted by Thoreau, who, when speaking of the double vision which presents itself to anyone who gazes into the water of a river;—first, the bottom, and then the sky beyond it,—said:—"We noticed that it required a separate intention of the eye, a more free and abstracted vision, to see the reflected trees and sky, than to see the river bottom merely. . . . Some men have their eyes naturally intended to the one, and some to the other object."*

What Melville really meant, in the paragraphs under consideration, is, that the whole book is but a compendium of *incomprehensible mysteries*, which would bear out my contention that *Moby Dick* is not *primarily*, but *superficially*, a tale of the sea.

Melville gives the reader ample invitation to look beneath the printed word. He advises him that "all these things are not without their meanings"; "it must symbolize something unseen"; "an

* A Week on the Concord and Merrimack Rivers.

[10]

allegory may lurk here"; or, "I must be content with a hint."

In further evidence of his cryptic way of working, he said; "Yet in some dim, random way, explain myself, I must, else all these chapters might be naught." He also treated his subject in a mysterious manner; he wrote in riddles; his method was indirect and ambiguous; he sought to convey ideas, without giving them definite expression; to hint; to suggest; to imply; to present the enigma of life in an enigmatic way, and to emphasize the mystery of the ineffable mysteries, for he believed it is "but vain to popularize profundities." Moreover, from an artistic standpoint, he understood the relation of obscurity to the sublime.

Symbolism, for Melville, was more than a mere playing with ideas, for there is an air of sincerity in his statement, that; "Some certain significance lurks in all things, else all things are of little worth, and the round world itself but an empty cipher." And also; "How immaterial are all materials. What real things are there but imponderable thoughts." Another line to the same effect is; "Methinks that what they call my shadow here on earth, is my true substance."*

To prove that Melville wrote in parables and symbols, we have a paragraph, with a double meaning, in which he states his intention to write a story

* Note 1.

[11]

with a double meaning; for, after summing up his reasons for going a-whaling, he concludes with the following admission:

"By reason of these things, then, the whaling voyage was welcome; the great flood-gates of the wonder world swung open, and in the wild conceits that swayed me to my purpose, two and two, there floated into my inmost soul, endless processions of the whale, and midmost of them all, one grand hooded phantom, like a snow hill in the air."

The above given paragraph is a typical example of Melville's literary legerdemain, with which he has so successfully deceived the mental eye of his readers. Nevertheless the clue to the hidden meaning may be found in the specific use of the words: —"*two and two,*" which describe the formation of the whales' grotesque parade.

In addition to the fact that two and two make four, the words; "two and two," reveal the secret plan of the book, for they connote; pairs, couples, duplicates, analogies, correspondences, representatives, parables, allegories, and symbols. "Endless processions," suggests the infinite scope of symbolism; "wild conceits," means exactly what the words denote, the possibilities of which he saw, when the "flood-gates of the wonder world,"—meaning his imagination,—"swung open." The "grand hooded phantom" in the middle, of course, was Moby Dick;

but his premature introduction weakens the plausibility of the superficial narrative.

Melville's appreciation of the mystic qualities of "two and two," is expressed in the following apostrophe:

"O Nature, and O soul of man! how far beyond all utterance are your linked analogies! not the smallest atom stirs or lives on matter, but has its cunning duplicate in mind."

The foregoing quotation is a close paraphrase of a passage in Swedenborg's *Doctrine of Correspondences*, which is as follows:

"It has been given me to know from much experience, that in the natural world, and its three kingdoms, there is not the smallest thing which does not represent something in the spiritual world, or which has not something there to which it corresponds."

Another proof of Melville's intention to make the superficial narrative, the vehicle for a darker story, is found in his impassioned supplication:—

"If then to meanest mariners, and renegades, and castaways, I shall hereafter ascribe high qualities, though dark; weave round them tragic graces; if even the most mournful, perchance the most abased among them all, shall at times lift himself to the exalted mounts; if I shall touch that workman's arm with some ethereal light; if I shall spread a rainbow over his disastrous set of sun;

then against all mortal critics bear me out in it, thou just Spirit of Equality, which has spread one royal mantle of humanity over all my kind. Bear me out in it, thou great democratic God, who didst not refuse to the swart convict, Bunyan, the pale poetic pearl; Thou who didst clothe with doubly hammered leaves of finest gold, the stumped and paupered arm of old Cervantes."

The future events hinted at in the foregoing paragraph, will be identified as they occur; but the immediate significance lies in the word *"dark,"* for it poetically describes the manner in which he will ascribe qualities to his characters. Furthermore, it should be recalled, that Bunyan was a master of religious allegory, and also that Cervantes invented an immortal crusade for the betterment of humanity, which accounts for Melville's petition to the "great democratic God" of genius, for support in creating the hidden allegorical crusade, which he had in mind.

Although Melville hinted frequently, that the reader should read between the lines, he guarded against any possible transparency in his design, with the following disclaimer:—

"I do not know where I can find a better place than just here, to make mention of one or two things, which to me seem important, as in printed form, establishing in all respects the reasonableness of the whole story of the White Whale, more espe-

cially the catastrophe. For this is one of those dis-
heartening instances where truth requires as much
bolstering as error. So ignorant are most landsmen of some of the plainest and most palpable
wonders of the world, that without some hints, historical and otherwise, of the fishery, they might
scout Moby Dick as a monstrous fable, or still
worse, and more detestable, a hideous and intolerable allegory."

All of the foregoing evasion, however, is merely
a stroke of finesse, intended to divert the reader
from the trail. But yet, there is some difference
among the meanings of fable, allegory, and parable.

A fable is not intended to be probable, or even
possible; it merely serves to teach a moral; an allegory treats of spiritual things in terms of the material world; but it should conceal nothing; it is not
intended to perplex the reader; but a parable describes something that might actually happen, and
it conveys a hidden spiritual meaning which is
parallel in sense with the obvious meaning. Therefore, to be exact, *Moby Dick* is a parable, which
Melville did not deny. Moreover, it may be said,
that when an allegory is hidden, it becomes a
parable.

But Melville also affirmed the literal meaning
of the story, for, according to report, a notoriously
vicious whale, called "Mocha Dick," did roam the

seas during the first half of the last century. An account of that whale states that:—

"From first to last, 'Mocha Dick' had nineteen harpoons put into him. He stove fourteen boats and caused the death of over thirty men. He stove three whaling vessels so badly that they were nearly lost, and he attacked and sunk a French merchantman and an Australian trader. He was encountered in every ocean and on every known feeding ground."*

Melville mentions several whales, by name, that had reputations for being terrors, in their time, but he does not mention "Mocha Dick," so it is possible that Melville used him for his material symbol, and modified the name to "Moby Dick."

The color of the whale may also be a historical fact, for we have recent proof that such freaks of nature may happen, as the following dispatch will show:—

"Washington, June 10 (1930 A.P.). An official report from Commander P. F. Roach, of the Coast Guard ship Modoc, to-day said a white whale had been sighted off the Newfoundland banks.

"Commander Roach said the white whale was swimming with a black one, and disappeared after making two short dives on its way past the ship."

However, the reader is given ample evidence

* Herman Melville, by John Freeman.

[16]

that the material story hides an allegory by the following indirect admission:

"The outblown rumors of the White Whale did in the end incorporate with themselves all manner of morbid hints, and half-formed foetal suggestions of supernatural agencies, which eventually invested Moby Dick with new terrors unborrowed from anything that visibly appears." And again: —"The hunt should in some way be stripped of that strange imaginative impiousness which naturally invested it; that the full terror of the voyage must be kept withdrawn into the obscure background."

It may be understood, then, that the superficial narrative is a cloak for the underlying story, and that the bond uniting the two, is the bond of *analogy*.

With regard to interpretation; there are two methods. The one which seems to have been invariably followed by the commentators on *Moby Dick*, is the subjective method, and the results are personal inventions. Such conclusions are purely arbitrary, and it follows, that the same subject would, naturally, be given a different meaning by each individual interpreter.

The other method is objective; for it is based upon facts ascertained from the text, that is, internal evidence, and the reasoning process is inductive, or progressing, by analogy, from what is known, to what is unknown.

A rule that may be applied to the unravelling of analogic fabrics, was formulated by Henry Fielding, who advised:—

"In discovering the deceit of others, it matters much that our own art, be wound up, if I may use the expression, in the same key with theirs, for very artful men sometimes miscarry by fancying others wiser than they really are."*

Similar advice for solving a problem which involves the mental workings of another person, is also submitted by Edgar Allan Poe:—

"The identification of the reasoner's intellect with that of his opponent's depends, upon the accuracy with which the opponent's intellect is measured. . . . When the cunning of the individual felon is diverse in character from their own, the felon foils them of course. This always happens when it is above their own, and very usually when it is below."†

Therefore, to uncover the hidden story, the reader should follow the same plane of thought pursued by Melville, in concealing it. Melville's intention and method should be clearly understood. His plan was definite and deliberate. He did not

* Tom Jones.
† The Purloined Letter.

[18]

write in a trance, as some interpretations would imply.

This required plane of thought is neither higher nor lower, than is necessary to a consistent method of hiding mystical doctrines in the words of material descriptions. "But in matters like this, subtlety appeals to subtlety, and without imagination, no man can follow another into these halls."

However, many of the subjects hinted at by Melville, are "too analytic to be verbally developed" and "which to explain, would be to dive deeper than Ishmael can go"; therefore I have avoided all allusions to esoteric cults and metaphysical pitfalls.

Some of the lines and paragraphs, surreptitiously interpolated into the text, and which conceal ulterior meanings, may, by the presence of absurdities, be easily detected; for in order to make some of the double meanings fit each other, Melville was forced far out of the path of probability or even plausibility.

Such instances may be regarded as positive proof of his intention to conceal ulterior meanings; but many suspicious paragraphs betray no clue; so the verity of the analogous hidden meanings in them, depends upon their consistency with Melville's general subject. Although this is not an exact process, the results are of as high a degree of probability, as it is possible to attain by an inductive method.

Objection may be made to interpretations of words and phrases taken from their context and apparently forced or twisted to fit ulterior meanings; but such sentences embody Melville's convictions of general truths, and they are interpolated as hints touching the hidden meaning of the book, to which they apply with even greater force, than they do to their own visible context, and it should be remembered that Lowell said:—"There is such a difference between far-reaching and far-fetching."

III

ALTHOUGH many symbols and omens, in *Moby Dick*, must speak for themselves, Melville did explain a number of them. An omen was seen in the accidental dropping overboard, of the speaking trumpet, by the captain of the *Albatross;* for,—"In various silent ways, the seamen were evincing their observance of this ominous incident." Another omen is suggested, when, at the same time;—"shoals of small harmless fish, that for some days had been placidly swimming by our side, darted away with what seemed shuddering fins." Starbuck saw an omen in the smashed whale boat, on the quarter-deck, for he said:—" 'Tis a solemn sight; an omen, and an ill one." He also saw an omen in the great live squid, and remarked:—"Few whale ships ever beheld it and returned to their ports to tell of it."

A symbol was pointed out in the episode of the lost whale boat, when Ishmael commented:— "There, then, he sat, holding up that imbecile candle in the midst of that almighty forlornness. There, then, he sat, the sign and symbol of a man without faith, hopelessly holding up hope in the midst of despair."

Another symbol was suggested by Melville, when, according to old English law, he inferred that a sturgeon's head was considered to be royal property:—"the king receiving the highly dense and elastic head, peculiar to that fish, which symbolically regarded, may possibly be humorously grounded upon some presumed congeniality."

A symbol was seen in:—"the wind that made great bellies of their sails, and rushed the vessel on by arms invisible as irresistible; this seemed the symbol of that unseen agency which so enslaved them to the race."

Another symbol was suggested when Ahab threw his pipe overboard, and said:—"What business have I with this pipe? This thing that is made for sereneness." Although the pipe symbol may be classed as silent, it is intended to show, emphatically, that *serenity* was incompatible with Ahab's troubled soul.

In speaking of the color, white, Melville said:—"It is at once the most meaning symbol of spiritual things." And a very important symbol, so far as this story is concerned, was revealed by Captain Ahab, when he happened to see Queequeg's coffin, and exclaimed:—"Here now's the very dreaded symbol of grim death." Other symbols are mentioned, such as:—"the evil blazing diamond, once the divinest symbol of the crystal skies"; and "the waif may be deemed the grand symbol and badge" (of the whale fishery).

Ishmael was forever looking for symbols and

omens, so when he arrived at the "Twy Pots, . . . one of the best kept hotels in all Nantucket," he remarked:—" 'It's ominous. . . . Tombstones staring at me in the whalemen's chapel; and here a gallows; and a pair of prodigious black pots too! Are these last throwing out oblique hints touching Tophet?' " Tombstones are another symbol of death, and what he also saw, was *sin* symbolized by the gallows, with the disconcerting idea of *hell*, suggested, symbolically, by the black pots. Captain Ahab had the same habit of looking for symbols and omens, for it is said of him:—"to any monomaniac man, the veriest trifles capriciously carry meanings."

IV

DESPITE Melville's gesture to discourage attempts to discover the symbolical correspondence of Moby Dick, a number of interpretations have been published.

Mr. Raymond M. Weaver* maintains:—"Yet fabulous allegory it is; an allegory of the demonism at the cankered heart of nature, teaching that, 'though in many of its visible aspects, the world seems formed in love, the invisible spheres were formed in fright.' Thou shalt know the truth, and the truth shall make you mad. To the eye of Truth, so Melville would convince us, 'the palsied universe lies before us like a leper.' . . . 'all deified Nature absolutely paints like a harlot, whose allurements cover nothing but the charnel house within.' To embody this devastating insight, Melville chooses as a symbol, an albino whale." Mr. Weaver also referred to Moby Dick, as "the monstrous symbol and embodiment of unconquerable evil."

Mr. John Freeman,† from various points of view, presents several solutions:—

"Ahab and the whale, the prototype of an eternal bloody strife between opposites. If you ask for

* Herman Melville, Mariner and Mystic.
† Herman Melville.

a definition of those opposites, the answer is not very easy. They are, in one view, spirit against flesh; eternity against time; in another view; pride against pride; madness against madness; unreason against unreason. Indeed the opposition is not an essential one, as Melville presents it; rather than a clashing of opposites, there is a contest of rivals. One matches the other, man and whale are alike vindictive and remorseless; the same nature, the same necessity urges both; the conflict has been set from the foundations of the world."

Mr. Freeman also believes:—"This is Melville's theme as it was Milton's, but the name of the great enemy is not Lucifer, but Leviathan. The never-to-be-ended combat typified by Milton's Lucifer and Archangels, is typified as boldly by Melville's Moby Dick and Captain Ahab. . . . It is a parable of an eternal strife."

"You may read it as a mere narrative of wonders, you may read it as an allegory of the ancient war between spirit and sense, or between the simple lust of domination and the more primitive lust of strength and freedom."

Dr. Carl Van Doren* is reluctant to admit that Melville wrote *Moby Dick* with any ulterior meaning in mind, as these lines will show:—

"Ahab who had lost a leg in the jaws of the

* A Short History of American Literature.

whale, is driven by a wild desire for revenge, which has maddened him, and which makes him identify Moby Dick with the very spirit of evil and hatred. Ahab, not Melville, is to blame, if the story seems an allegory, which Melville plainly declares it is not; but it contains, nevertheless, the semblance of a conflict between the ancient and unescapable forces of nature and the ineludable enmity of man."

In *Lucifer from Nantucket*,* Dr. Van Doren takes an opposite view to that of Mr. Freeman, and thinks:—"Ahab is the Yankee Faust, the Yankee Lucifer. . . . Nor was it merely Lucifer in Ahab, which Melville comprehended. He saw him also, in some degree, as Faust, bound to get at the truth though it should blast him. . . . The spirit of all whalers, the spirit of all sailors, yes, the spirit of all dauntless men, seems matched against the spirit of resisting, malicious nature, personified in Moby Dick." Dr. Van Doren also assures us that: —"How far Melville meant Moby Dick to be a symbol, cannot now be discovered."

Dr. Henry Seidel Canby† finds that:—"Melville, friend of Hawthorne, and transcendentalist philosopher on his own account, sees nature as greater and more terrible than man. He sees the will of man trying to control the universe, but fail-

* Century Magazine, 1925.
† Everday Americans.

ing; crushed if uncowed by the unmeasured power of an evil nature, which his little spirit, once it loses touch with the will of God, vainly encounters."

Mr. Percy H. Boynton,* thinks:—"This is the story of Eve and Prometheus, the perennial story of man's struggle for spiritual victory in the midst of a world of harassing circumstances, and in the midst of a world where fate opposes the individual in the form of his own thwarting self." Concerning symbols, Mr. Boynton believes:—"The ocean is the boundless truth; the land the threatening reef of human error. . . . The whale is the symbol of all property and privileges."

Mr. Herbert Gorman† opines that the whale "was the passionate, deceptive, cruel all-conquering world, and Herman Melville was the eternal sailor, the divine adventurer, urging his ship ever a little further toward the uncompromising monster that rules the deeps of time."

Mr. Fred Lewis Pattee,‡ thinks:—"Melville was a Nietzschean when Nietzsche was but a schoolboy. Be hard, smite down, trample, be a superman, or else be yourself trampled—that was the law of Nature,—of God, if there be a God . . . it bursts upon you that this is more than a mere voyage; it is an infernal Pilgrim's progress; it is a

* Contemporary Americans.
† N. Y. Times Book Review, Mar. 10, 1929.
‡ American Mercury, 1927.

study of the fundamentals of human life; it is a clinic; it is a mad attempt to thrust aside the veil that hides the supreme mystery of man; it is a mad 'Invictus' hurled at 'whatever gods there be.' "

Mr. D. H. Lawrence,* insists, concerning Moby Dick:—"Of course he is a symbol.

"Of what?

"I doubt if even Melville knew exactly.

"That's the best of it.

". . . It is an epic of the sea, such as no man has equalled; and it is a book of esoteric symbolism of profound significance and of considerable tiresomeness. . . .

"What then is Moby Dick?—He is the deepest blood-being of the white race. He is our deepest blood-nature. And he is hunted, hunted, hunted by the maniacal fanaticism of our white mental consciousness. We want to hunt him down. To subject him to our will. . . .

"The last phallic being of the white man. Hunted into the death of upper-consciousness and the ideal will. Our blood consciousness sapped by a parasitic or ideal consciousness."

Mr. Lewis Mumford,† presents an exhaustive exposition of the mystery, from several different angles.

"Moby Dick is a portrait of the whale and a

* Studies in American Classic Literature.
† Herman Melville.

presentation of the demonic energies of the universe that harass and frustrate and extinguish the spirit of man. . . . Moby Dick is a labyrinth, and that labyrinth is the universe . . .

"The whale is no phantom symbol; and this stage is no pasteboard stage. If this is not the universe, the full universe, that Melville embodies under the symbols, no one in our time has had an inkling of a fuller one. . . .

"Moby Dick is an imaginative synthesis; and every aspect of reality belongs to it, one plane modifying the other and creating the modelled whole. . . . Ahab is a reality in relation to Moby Dick; and when Melville projects him, he ceases to be incredible, because he is alive. . . .

"Although the savage harpooners get nearest the whale, the savage universe, it is Ahab and the Parsee, the European and the Asiatic, who carry the pursuit to its ultimate end—while a single American survives to tell the tale.

"What is the meaning of *Moby Dick?* There is not one meaning; there are many; but in its simplest terms, *Moby Dick* is, necessarily a story of the sea and its ways, as the Odyssey is a story of strange adventures, and *War and Peace* a story of battles and domestic life.

"But *Moby Dick*, admirable as it is as a narrative of maritime adventure, is far more than that; it is, fundamentally a parable on the mystery of evil and the accidental malice of the universe. The White Whale stands for the brute energies of existence, blind, fatal, overpowering, while Ahab is the spirit of man, small and feeble, but purposive, that pits its puniness against this might, and its purpose against the blank senseless power. . . .

"The White Whale is the symbol of that persistent force of destruction, that meaningless force, which now figures as the out-pouring of a volcano or the atmospheric disruption of a tornado, or again, as the mere aimless dissipation of unused energy into an unavailable void—that spectacle which so disheartened the learned Henry Adams.

"In Moby Dick, Melville conquered the White Whale in his own consciousness; instead of blankness, there was significance; instead of aimless energy, there was purpose, and instead of random living, there was life. . . . Not tame and gentle bliss, but disaster, heroically encountered, is man's true happy ending. . . . In another sense, The Whale stands for the practical life.

"There, it seems to me, is another meaning in Ahab's struggle with Moby Dick. He represents, not as in the first parable, an heroic power that misconceives its mission and misapplies itself; here he rather stands for human purpose in its highest expression.

"Each man will read into *Moby Dick* the drama of his own experience and that of his contemporaries. . . . Mr. Van Wyck Brooks has found in the White Whale an image like that of Grendel in Beowulf, expressing the Northern consciousness of the hard fight against the elements; while for the disciple of Jung, the White Whale is the symbol of the unconscious, which torments man, and yet is the source of his proudest efforts."

Mr. Ernest Rhys,* remarks, concerning Melville;—"He was not only a writer of sea tales, but a transcendentalist in oilskin, who found a vaster ocean than the Pacific in his own mind, and symbolized in the whale the colossal image of the forces of nature that produce and that overpower man."

Mr. E. L. Grant Watson is quoted by Mr. Weaver, as follows:—"It is Mr. Watson's contention in this essay,† that the *Pequod* with her monomaniac captain and all his crew, is representative of Melville's own genius, and in the particular sense that each character is deliberately symbolic of a complete and separate element."

In a later essay,‡ Mr. Watson discovers that Melville's *Pierre* and *Moby Dick* are founded upon another theme. In speaking of *Pierre*, he said:—

"It is the story of a conscious soul attempting to draw itself free from the psychic world-material in

* Everymans' Library Edition 1922.
† London Mercury, Dec. 1920.
‡ New England Quarterly, June 1930.

which most of mankind is unconsciously always wrapped and enfolded, as a foetus in the womb. Melville would draw the history and the tragedy of a soul seeking freedom outside, (or rather apart from,) the world-substance. And here we find an analogy in the book which immediately precedes *Pierre*.

"In this comparison we see that, as the mysterious Isabel is a danger and a final destruction to the virtuous Pierre, (Pierre who is Melville's representation of the God-man,) so the mysterious White Whale in *Moby Dick* is a danger and ultimate destruction to Ahab and all his crew, (Ahab being the Man-god.)*

"Isabel is of the same world-substance (mother substance) as Moby Dick; the aspect from which they are viewed constituting the difference. Their mystery, their attractiveness and their all-engulfing destructiveness is the same. If we have understood the books aright, we see them as complementary aspects of the same problem. And here again it should be emphasized that Isabel is no more a symbol of *evil*, than is the White Whale. In both these books Melville is dealing with life-values which are beyond good and evil. Only from the terrestrial human standpoint, and still enwrapped in that same mother-substance of the world, do these words have any meaning."

* Note 2.

Mr. John Erskine* believes that:—"The story becomes a parable of Man's agony to unite himself with what is universal, with the infinite, as man links infinity in nature, in time and in space. . . . The whale is the image of the sea, if you choose, of this mysterious and terrible space, but the sea is the image of nothing but itself." Read that last sentence over again, it is worth the trouble.

Mr. H. M. Tomlinson† provides the climax to the foregoing symposium, in the following words:—

"The whale which was hunted by Captain Ahab and the men of Nantucket, was a more wonderful quarry than all the oceans of this world could hold. That mythical whale left this earth, and, a gigantic but elusive shadow, it led those men up among the stars. The good ship, *Pequod*, navigated the constellations in pursuit of it and hurled spears, so to speak, at the Great Bear."

Melville also found the subject too big for this world, as his words imply:—

"Nor when expandingly lifted by your subject, can you fail to trace out great whales in the starry heavens, and boats in pursuit of them; . . . Thus at the North have I chased Leviathan round and round the Pole. . . . And beneath the effulgent Antarctic skies I have boarded the *Argo Navis*, and joined the chase against the starry Cetus far be-

* The Delineator, Oct. 1929.
† Harper's Magazine, 1926.

yond the utmost stretch of Hydrus and the Flying Fish."

The significant merit that may be accorded the foregoing varied and contradictory interpretations, is, they all agree that the White Whale symbolizes a mystery. On this point, if on no other, there is entire unanimity.

In further proof that Moby Dick contains a hidden meaning, the following letter is submitted. This letter is from Herman Melville to Mrs. Nathaniel Hawthorne, and is dated, New York, January 8, 1852.

"I have hunted up the finest Bath [paper] I could find, gilt-edged and stamped, whereon to indite my humble acknowledgement of your highly flattering letter.

". . . It really amazed me that you should find any satisfaction in that book. It is true that some men have said they were pleased with it, but you are the only woman. . . . But, then, since you, with your spiritualizing nature, see more things than other people, and by the same process, refine all you see, so that they are not the same things that other people see, but things, which while you think you but humbly discover them, you do in fact create them for yourself—therefore, upon the whole, I do not so much marvel at your expressions concern'g Moby Dick. At any rate, your allusion for example to the 'spirit spout' first showed to me

that there was a subtle significance in that thing—
but I did not, in that case mean it. I had some
vague idea while writing it, that the whole book
was susceptible of an allegorical construction, and
also that parts of it were—but the specialty of
many of the particular subordinate allegories were
first revealed to me after reading Mr. Hawthorne's
letter, which, without citing any particular ex-
amples, yet intimated the part-and-parcel allegori-
calness of the whole.—But my Dear Lady, I shall
not again send you a bowl of salt water. The next
chalice I shall commend will be a rural bowl of
milk. . . .

". . . Does Mr. Hawthorne continue his calls
upon all his neighbors within a radius of ten miles?
Shall I send him ten packs of visiting cards? . . .
He goes into society too much altogether. . . .
Now, Madam, had you not said anything about
Moby Dick, and had Mr. Hawthorne been equally
silent, then had I said, perhaps, something to both
of you about another Wonder-(-full) Book. But
as it is, I must be silent. How is it that while all of
us human beings are so entirely disembarrassed in
censuring a person, that so soon as we would praise,
then we begin to feel awkward? I never blush
after denouncing a man, but I grow scarlet after
eulogizing him. And yet this is all wrong; and
yet we can't help it. . . .

"Life is a long Dardanelles, My Dear Madam,

the shores whereof are bright with flowers which we want to pluck, but the bank is too high; and so we float on and on, hoping to come to a landing place at last—but swoop! we launch into the great sea! Yet the geographers say, even then we must not despair, because across the great sea, however desolate and vacant it may look, lie all Persia and the delicious lands roundabout Damascus. . . ."

The general character of the above given letter, is ambiguous and non-committal; for it would be quite natural that a matchless artist, such as Melville, would not be guilty of anticlimax, by exposing, or even admitting the hidden meanings in *Moby Dick*. It is art to conceal art, and Melville accomplished that end in his work; and he also guarded the secret of his book; for there is ground for suspicion in the fact that none of Mr. Hawthorne's letters to Herman Melville is known to exist.

It should also be understood that the flattering tribute paid to Mrs. Hawthorne, accrediting her with unconscious subjectivity, is a polite evasion. However, the cardinal point upon which Mr. Hawthorne, Mrs. Hawthorne, and Herman Melville agree, is that; "the whole book was susceptible of an allegorical construction."

The question of conscious versus unconscious symbolism is a problem in probabilities, and the answer depends upon the preponderance of probability one way, or the other. Now, as an ambiguity is neither an affirmation nor a denial, it is extremely probable, in view of Melville's own conviction, that it is "but vain to popularize profundities," that he should hint at such things, by means of symbols and parables, deliberately; and therefore, *consciously*.

The last paragraph of the foregoing letter is a good example of Melville's ability to write with a double meaning in his words, for, in a short description of worldly travel, he has compressed a complete parable of life, and death, and the hope of heaven.

V

IT is evident that the reviewers who have brought about the revival of interest in the works of Herman Melville are, in a general way, of the opinion that Moby Dick is symbolical of everything that is inimical to man. The fact that the White Whale symbolized a *principal* that is malevolent toward mankind can hardly be questioned, inasmuch as Melville insisted upon it, himself, plainly, and repeatedly. Moby Dick "might have seemed the gliding great demon of the seas of life," and he was definitely called "that intangible malignity that has been from the beginning."

The problem which Melville left for his readers to solve, is to specifically identify that principal. Melville had a clear idea of his normal subject, so it is not impossible to follow its hidden trail, if the necessary clues are detected, for "it may well be doubted whether human ingenuity can construct an enigma of the kind which human ingenuity may not, by proper application, resolve."*

Before proceeding with my own interpretation, it may be well to forestall any charge of coloring my conclusions with subjective theories; by stating that I am not a Swedenborgian, or a fatalist, or a mystic, of any description.

* The Gold Bug, Edgar Allan Poe.

Now, the supreme power which is given credit for being responsible for everything that happens in the universe,—the irresistible, irrational power that determines all events, with no manifest connection with reason or righteousness,—is FATE; *and Melville's symbol for Fate, is the White Whale.* Melville symbolized the responsible *first cause* of all human suffering; natural forces are only the *means* through which the so-called decrees of Fate are executed, and the resulting conditions are *effects.*

The meaning of Melville's rhapsody, previously quoted, becomes clear, when; "thoughts of this Leviathan (Fate) include the whole circle of the sciences, and all generations of whales, and men, and mastodons, past, present, and to come, with all the revolving panoramas of empire on earth, and throughout the whole universe."

Melville wrote a book about Fate, and all that it implies, without disclosing the identity of his subject. His text was; "wonderfullest things are ever the unmentionable," and he followed it consistently. He stated his position to Hawthorne, in a letter, as quoted by Mr. Weaver:*—"This is the book's motto, (the secret one,) *Ego non baptisto ti in nomine*—but make out the rest for yourself." In other words, the subject of the book was un-

* Herman Melville, Mariner and Mystic.

[39]

speakable, and Hawthorne was invited to discover, for himself, what it was all about.

Therefore, all of Melville's allusions to the White Whale, as being the symbol of Fate are indirect and suggestive. It was hinted that Moby Dick is "not only ubiquitous, but immortal," and Fate is implied, when, "the whale which from side to side, [was] strangely vibrating his predestinating head."

A hint is given when Tashtego, aloft, sighted the first whale;—"he stood hovering above you half suspended in air, so wildly and eagerly peering towards the horizon, you would have thought him some prophet or seer, beholding the shadows of Fate, and by those wild cries, announcing their coming."

A very close analogy to Fate is suggested by the detailed description of the anatomy and habits of the whale, because, altogether, they connote the attributes of a power that is blind, senseless, brainless, capricious, malignant, and indomitable.

The omnipresence of Fate, and the universal subjection of mankind to Fate, are hidden in the words;—"all men are enveloped in whale lines . . . and if you be a philosopher, though seated in the whale boat, you would not at heart feel more of terror, than though seated before your own evening fire, with a poker, and not a harpoon, by your side." Now, as a whale line is an emblem of the whale, it suggests Fate; and the concluding lines are a very pointed lesson in fatalism.

Another instance in which the whale line serves as an emblem of the whale, was observed by Captain Ahab, when the carpenter was at work, converting Queequeg's coffin into a lifebuoy. "See," said Ahab, "that thing rests on two line tubs, full of tow lines. A most malicious wag, that fellow."

Ahab saw the significance of the coffin;—symbol of *death*, supported by the emblems of the symbol of *Fate*, and he therefore gave the carpenter credit for perpetrating a gruesome, symbolical joke.

Fate is accused of injustice, when Captain Ahab addressed the whale's head:—

"Thou saw'st the locked lovers when leaping from their flaming ship, heart to heart they sank beneath the exulting wave; true to each other, when heaven seemed false to them. Thou saw'st the murdered mate when tossed by pirates from the midnight deck; for hours he fell into the deeper midnight of the insatiate maw; and his murderers still sailed on unharmed—while swift lightnings shivered the neighboring ship that would have borne a righteous husband to outstretched longing arms."

The same charge of injustice, with reference to the well-known Biblical victim, is implied in the line:—"Here was this grey-headed, ungodly old man, chasing a Job's whale around the world."

Furthermore, Melville mentions "the sperm whale, guided by some infallible instinct—say rather, secret intelligence from the Deity."

The relation of the whale to Fate, may be seen plainly, if the word *Fate* is substituted for the words, *"the whale."* "I am horror struck at this antemosaic, unsourced existence of the unspeakable terrors of the whale [Fate], which, having been before all time, must need exist after all human ages are over."

Although the foregoing quotations are rather plain hints that the whale is the symbol of Fate, the following paragraph, in shrouded language, contains evidence that is almost direct.

"In the great sperm whale, this high and mighty god-like dignity, inherent in the brow, is so immensely amplified, that gazing on it, in that full front view, you feel the Deity and the dread powers more forcibly than in beholding any other object in living nature. For you see no one point precisely . . . nothing but that one broad firmament of a forehead, plaited with riddles; dumbly lowering with the doom of boats, and ships, and men."

Almost every word in the above-given passage is suggestive of omnipotence; but it is the curious use of the word "firmament," in describing a whale's head, that gives us an unmistakable clue to the hidden meaning, or parallelism, in the paragraph; because, in this instance, Melville makes use of the most ancient conception of the Deity, for, "firmament" is synonymous with "sky" or "heaven."

"Now the Greek *Zeu*, the Latin *Deus*, (whence the French *Dieu*, and our *Deity*,) the Lithuanian *Diewas*, and the Sanskrit *Dyaus*, all come from an old Aryan root *div*, or *dyu*, meaning 'to shine.' The Sanskrit *dyu*, as a noun, means 'sky' or 'day,' and in the Veda, *Dyaus* is the bright sky or heaven. . . . But the Greek in whose Pantheon, Zeus had been exalted as god of gods, did not dream that to his remote ancestor, that god was but the sky personified and deified."*

The riddles mentioned, are the riddles of the universe; and the sky or "firmament," as well as the whale's brow, dumbly lowers with the doom of boats, and ships, and men. Moreover, it should be considered, that in observing the sky, "you see no one point precisely."

Another link uniting the Whale with Fate is in the question;—"How may unlettered Ishmael hope to read the awful Chaldee of the Sperm Whale's brow?"

Chaldee, as used here, means the astrological theories of those ancient people, the Chaldeans, who were the first to study the heavens, and who believed that the stars controlled the destinies of men and nations.

* The Birth and Growth of Myth, Edward Clodd, F.R.A.S.

This question is followed by the statement;—"I put that brow before you. Read it if you can."

Seeing that *Moby Dick* contains so much that is double in meaning, this announcement may be a challenge to the reader to interpret what Melville has set before him, as well as an invitation to read the heavens. The foregoing excerpts prove, conclusively, that Melville selected the Sperm Whale for the symbol of Fate, and Moby Dick was the idealized representative of his species.

The Fate motif appears, with variations, throughout the book. The first instance is found in the lines:

"But wherefore it was that after having repeatedly smelt the sea as merchant sailor, I should now take it into my head to go on a whaling voyage; this, the invisible police officer of the Fates, who has constant surveillance of me, and secretly dogs me, and influences me in some unaccountable way—he can better answer than anyone else."

Another reference to Fate is made, when Starbuck felt himself committed to Ahab's scheme, and he mused:—"Will I, Nill I, the ineffable thing has tied me to him; tows me with a cable I have no knife to cut." But jolly Stubb, in the same predicament, laughed it off, and remarked;—"Come what will, one comfort's always left—that unfailing comfort is, it's all predestinated." And again,

—"such a crew, so officered, seemed specially picked and packed by some infernal fatality."

In the chapter entitled, "The Mat Maker," another reference is found, for to Ishmael, "it seemed as if this were the loom of Time, and I myself were a shuttle, mechanically weaving away at the Fates." Fate is implied in the question by Ahab:—

"What is it, what nameless, inscrutable, unearthly thing is it; what cozening, hidden lord and master,.and cruel, remorseless emperor commands me; that against all natural lovings and longings, I so keep pushing, and crowding, and jamming myself on all the time; recklessly making me ready to do what in my own proper, natural heart, I durst not so much as dare?"

Upon the first sight of the White Whale, Ahab exclaimed;—"Fate reserved the doubloon for me. I only; none of ye could have raised the White Whale first." And then, when all the men became frenzied in the chase;—"the hand of Fate had snatched all their souls," and they "were all directed to that fatal goal."

In answer to Starbuck's pleading to desist from the chase, Ahab answered;—"Fool. I am Fate's lieutenant; I act under orders." Again, when, "a fatalistic despair . . . passed over the Parsee's face," and, "as for the men, though some of them lowly rumbled, their fear of Ahab was greater than their fear of Fate."

When Ahab's special harpoon was made;—"pole, iron and rope—like the Three Fates—remained inseparable." Another instance is found in the line;—"you then saw Ahab in all his fatal pride." Other allusions to Fate are found in the phrases;—"a mysterious fatality," "accursed fate," "the predestinated day arrived," "mortals ready and ripe for their fate." When the ship started on her voyage; "we . . . blindly plunged like fate into the lone Atlantic." Another instance is found in the line;—"the captain and crew become practical fatalists," and, finally;—"By heaven man, we are turned round and round in this world like yonder windlass, and Fate is the handspike."

In view of the cumulative evidence that *Moby Dick* is saturated with fatalism, it may seem strange that the leading character, the symbol of Fate, should have so completely escaped detection; but the perfect concealment of the spiritual correspondence of the White Whale, may be accounted for by the following episode, in which Captain Ahab demanded how the ship was heading.

" 'East-sou' east, sir,' said the frightened steersman.

" 'Thou liest!' smiting him with his clenched fist. 'Heading east at this hour in the morning, and the sun astern?' Upon this every soul was confounded; for the phenomenon just observed by Ahab had unaccountably escaped every one else; but its very blinding palpableness must have been the cause."

The effectiveness of what may paradoxically be termed; *open concealment, by blinding palpableness* is convincingly presented by Edgar Allan Poe, in a short story, entitled; *The Purloined Letter*. This story tells of an important letter which the police of Paris made every effort to possess. They probed every cubic inch of the apartment of the minister, who had stolen the letter, and they exhausted every resource of their professional skill in making searches.

However, the police failed to find it, because, as Poe states;—"To conceal this letter, the minister had resorted to the comprehensive and sagacious expedient of not attempting to conceal it at all."

The underlying principle of this psychological trick, is explained by Poe, with this illustration:—

"The over-largely lettered signs and placards of the street, escape observation by dint of being excessively obvious; and the physical oversight is precisely analogous with the moral inapprehension by which the intellect suffers to pass unnoticed those considerations which are too obtrusively and too palpably self-evident."

Likewise, by keeping the idea of Fate constantly in the mind of the reader, the true correspondence of the White Whale is hidden by its *blinding palpableness*, and so each reader overlooks it, and invents his own symbolical meaning for Moby Dick.

VI

FIGURATIVE language was used by Melville at every opportunity. The world is mentioned twice, metaphorically, in the following dialogue, wherein Ahab asked the carpenter;—
" 'What's that? there's now a patched professor in Queen Nature's granite founded college. . . . Where wert thou born?'

" 'In the little rocky Isle of Man, sir.'

" 'Excellent! Thou'st hit the world by that.' "

The world is also represented, in several instances, by an *inn*, and that symbol is used when Ishmael said:—" 'I am quite content if the world is ready to board and lodge me while I am putting up at this grim sign of The Thunder Cloud.' " This same symbol, an inn, is used elsewhere, and will be noticed. But the more important symbol for the world,—the symbol that takes its proper place in the hidden allegory, is the *ship*. Ishmael discovered this one, himself, when in his chapel meditation, he concluded;—" 'Yes, the world's a ship, on its passage out.' "

The analogy between the world and a ship, is implied in the phrase:—"frigate earth"; and also when Stubb wondered "whether the world is anchored anywhere." Ahab, in one of his complaints, combined the analogy of the world to a ship, with the analogy of men to leaky casks:—

" 'I'm all aleak myself. Aye leaks in leaks, not only full of leaky casks, but those leaky casks are in a leaky ship; and that's a far worse plight than the Pequod's, man.' "

Ishmael gave a good description of the world, from a pessimistic point of view, when he described the ship which he had selected for his voyage.

Both the eastern and the western hemispheres were represented in this symbolical ship; for her hull was built in America, and her masts were cut in Japan. Moreover, she was very old. "Her ancient decks were worn and wrinkled . . . her venerable bows looked bearded . . . she was a thing of trophies—a cannibal of a craft, . . . a noble craft; but somehow a most melancholy."

The relation of Fate to the world was represented by bones of the Whale, with which the ship was abundantly furnished. "Her bulwarks were garnished like one continuous jaw, with the long, sharp teeth of the sperm whale . . . and the tiller was in one mass, curiously carved from the lower jaw of her hereditary foe." All of which signifies that *the world is encompassed by Fate;* and that *the world is controlled by Fate;* and also, that *Fate is inimical to the world.*

Her name, *Pequod,* was the name of a tribe of Indians; "now extinct as the ancient Medes";

therefore, it symbolized *Time;* and the blank waste, into which Ishmael gazed, at the suggestion of Captain Peleg, and of which "the prospect was unlimited, but exceedingly monotonous and forbidding"; and into which the ship was destined to sail; is a fitting symbol of *Space.*

This symbolical ship was manned by personifications of the virtues and vices, and also of the moral and spiritual qualities of mankind. Captain Ahab, in his capacity of commander, personified the *Ego,* the *Will,* the *Soul,* and the *Intellect.*

The short parable identifying the *Intellect,* and asserting its superiority to material things, is in the lines:—

" 'Ahab's above the common; Ahab's been in colleges, as well as 'mong cannibals; been used to deeper wonders than the waves; fixed his fiery lance in mightier, stranger foes than whales' "; meaning that the intellect grapples with, and probes the profound mysteries of life and destiny.

Ahab's personification of the *Ego,* is revealed when he read the symbols on the gold doubloon:— " 'There's something ever egotistical in mountain tops and towers, and all other grand and lofty things; look here,—three peaks proud as Lucifer. The firm tower, that is Ahab; the volcano; that is Ahab; the courageous, the undaunted, and victorious fowl, that, too, is Ahab; all are Ahab.' "

The *Soul* was identified with Ahab, by Elijah,

"the prophet of the wharves," as Ishmael called him. Elijah gave mysterious hints concerning the doubtful character of the proposed voyage, and, referring to Captain Ahab, said;—" 'He's got enough (soul) to make up for all deficiencies in other chaps.' " Moreover, the captain also said of himself;—" 'Ahab's soul's a centipede that moves upon a hundred legs.' "

The *Will* is presented in the description of Ahab's determination, as follows:—

"The path to my fixed purpose is laid with iron rails, whereon my Soul is grooved to run. Over unsounded gorges, through the rifled hearts of mountains, under torrents' beds, unerringly I rush. Naught's an obstacle, naught's an agle to the iron way."

But an interesting restriction was attached to the personification of the *Will;* for Captain Ahab had an artificial leg, which was made of whale ivory, and, that being an emblem of the Whale, it signifies that *the Will is limited by Fate.*

An artificial leg, made of whale ivory, is a typical absurdity introduced for its symbolical value; for a leg made of white oak would not only weigh less than half as much as an ivory leg; but it would be considerably stronger. Three ivory legs were broken, in the course of the story; one before the ship sailed, and two at sea; which at least is plausible.

Ishmael discovered the limitation of the will, when he analyzed his reasons for going a-whaling. His conclusion was:—

"I believe I can see a little into the springs and motives which being cunningly presented to me, under various disguises, induced me to set about performing the part I did, besides cajoling me into the deulsion that it was a choice resulting from my own unbiased free will and discriminating judgement."

Melville mentions the fact that free will is limited, in the chapter; "The Mat Maker";— "The straight warp of necessity, not to be swerved from its ultimate course . . . free will still free to ply her shuttle between given threads. . . ." And he regretfully admitted it, when Ishmael said:— "I seemed distinctly to perceive . . . that my free will had received a mortal wound."

The ivory leg served as a symbol of *death*, also, for Melville was deeply impressed by the contrast between life and death, and he brought those two ideas in juxtaposition, frequently. The leg symbol was used when "Ahab trampled his quadrant with his live and dead feet." And again;—"On life and death this old man walked." The same idea is presented in the words;—"Life folded Death; Death trellised Life," and "Oh lonely death on lonely life." It is also parabolically hidden in the phrase;—"excavating an old city grave yard, for the foundations of a Lying-in Hospital."

The three mates, Starbuck, Stubb, and Flask, are representatives, or personifications of three of the Greek schools of philosophy, among which mankind is divided, in a general way.

Starbuck, the chief mate, personified *Platonism*, for he was:—"a staid, steadfast man whose life for the most part was a telling pantomime of action, and not a tame chapter of sounds. Yet, for all his hardy sobriety and fortitude, there were certain qualities in him which at times affected, and in some cases seem well-nigh to over-balance all the rest. Uncommonly conscientious for a seaman, and endued with a deep natural reverence, the wild watery loneliness of his life did therefore strongly incline him to superstition, which in some organizations seems rather to spring, somehow, from intelligence than from ignorance. Outward portents and inward presentiments were his."

When Starbuck read the symbols on the doubloon, he found;—"A dark valley between three mighty heaven-abiding peaks, that almost seem the Trinity, in some faint earthly symbol. So in this vale of Death, God girds us round; and over all our gloom, the Sun of Righteousness still shines a beacon and a hope." The finding of faith, hope, and righteousness, by Starbuck, is a slant toward *Platonism*.

Stubb, the second mate, personified *Epicurean-ism,* as plainly appears in the analysis of his character:—

"A happy-go-lucky; neither craven nor valiant, taking perils as they come, with an indifferent air; and while engaged in the most imminent crises of the chase, toiling away, calm and collected as a journeyman joiner engaged for the year. Good-humored, easy and careless, he presided over his whale boat as if the most deadly encounter were but a dinner, and his crew all invited guests. He was as particular about the comfortable arrangement of his part of the boat, as an old stage driver is about the snugness of his box. . . . Long usage had, for this Stubb, converted the jaws of death into an easy chair. What he thought of death itself, there is no telling. Whether he ever thought of it at all, might be a question."

On one occasion, Stubb remarked;—"I guess he's got what some folks ashore call a conscience . . . I don't know what it is," and he also said;—"Think not, is my eleventh commandment."

When Stubb inspected the doubloon, his first thought was of the possibility of having a good time with it, for, "Stubb was a high liver," and he said;—"Which did I have it now on Negro Hill or in Corlaer's Hook, I'd not look at it very long ere spending it." And when he saw the signs of the zodiac, on the doubloon, he thought they represented the comedy of life; and his final remark was;—"Oh jolly's the word for aye." In other words;—'Pleasure is the sovereign good'; the creed of the *Epicurean*. Stubb is quite definitely classified, when he "heeded not the mumblings of the banquet that was going on so nigh him, no more than the sharks heeded the smacking of his own epicurean lips."

In the light of the interpretations of these two characters, a meaning may be found in the following obscure speech, by Captain Ahab:—"Starbuck —Stubb, ye two are the opposite poles of one thing, Starbuck is Stubb reversed, and Stubb is Starbuck, (reversed) and ye two are all mankind." This means that all mankind is included between the two extremes of human nature;—Spirituality, which is the highest quality, and Sensuality, which is the lowest quality.

The third mate, Flask, personified *Stoicism*. He was thoroughly practical and unimaginative. When he read the symbols on the doubloon, he said:—"I see nothing here, but a round thing made of gold, and whoever raises a certain whale, this round thing belongs to him. . . . It is worth sixteen dollars, that's true."

The incompatibility of the Epicurean point of view, with that of the Stoic, is expressed by Stubb, who, overhearing Flask, said:—"Shall I call that wise or foolish now; if it be really wise, it has a foolish look to it; yet if it be really foolish, then it has a sort of wiseish look to it."

Flask also possessed the Stoic's sense of responsibility, for, at the catastrophe, his last words were: —"O Stubb, I hope my poor mother's drawn my part pay ere this; if not, few coppers will come to her now, for the voyage is up."

It is said of Flask, that:—"So utterly lost was he to all sense of reverence for the many marvels of their majestic bulk and mystic ways; and so dead to anything like apprehension of any possible danger from encountering them, that in his poor opinion, the wondrous whale was but a species of magnified mouse, or at least, water-rat." This conforms closely to the teaching of Epictetus, who said:—"Men are disturbed not by the things which happen, but by the opinions about the things."*

Although Melville did not approve of the Stoics, he gave that division of mankind credit for certain valuable qualities, as follows:—

"As carpenter's nails are divided into wrought nails and cut nails; so mankind may be similarly divided. Little Flask was one of the wrought ones; made to clinch tight and last long. They called him 'King-post,' on board the *Pequod;* because in form he could be well likened to the short, square timber known by that name in Arctic whalers; and which by means of many radiating

* The Discourses of Epictetus.

[56]

side timbers inserted into it, serves to brace the ship against the icy concussions of those battering seas."

Melville's aptitude for seeing analogies is shown here, first, by comparing the Stoic with a wrought nail, and then symbolizing the Stoic, by the silent symbol, "King-post." And a very fitting one it is, for it holds its place in the *ship*,—symbol of the *world*,—four-square against all adversity; patiently, unflinchingly, doing its duty, and supporting the world by its practical services.

Next in importance, come the harpooners, of whom Queequeg is the first, and who personifies *Religion*.

As religion is an important topic, in this book of parables and hidden allegories, it may be well to examine into the fitness of a savage, pagan cannibal serving as the personification of *Religion*. But it should be considered, that the term; religion, includes all forms of religion, and therefore, its personification should cover as much ground as possible, and represent all phases of religion.

Ishmael's liking for Queequeg, as shown by the many favorable comments on his personality, means that Melville had a sincere regard for natural religion,—that is, for religion in its pristine character, as it would be practiced by a primitive man. He said, speaking of Queequeg;—"He no doubt thought he knew a good deal more about the true religion than I did."

The worship of the little idol, Yojo, and the vigil and the fast of the "ramadan," represent the complex ceremonies with which simple religion is overlaid; and the cannibal quality of Queequeg, gives a hint of Melville's cynical opinion of the doctrine of transubstantiation.

The Christian religion, in Melville's opinion, did not compare favorably with primitive, or natural religion, as may be seen in the numerous instances wherein he notes the superiority of the latter.

The first instance is in the line;—"Better sleep with a sober cannibal than a drunken Christian." And in his appraisal of Queequeg, he said;—"You cannot hide the soul . . . I thought I saw traces of a simple honest heart, and in his large, deep eyes, fiery black and bold, there seemed tokens of a spirit that would dare a thousand devils. And besides all this, there was a certain lofty bearing about the pagan, which even his uncouthness could not altogether maim."

Melville also said;—"He (Queequeg) looked like a man who had never cringed and never had a creditor." This means that true religion submits to no ecclesiastical authority, and owes nothing to a vicarious agent. Melville said further, in the words of Ishmael;—"I'll try a pagan friend, thought I, since Christian kindness has proved but hollow courtesy."

The contaminating effect of sojourning among Christians, is more than implied in Queequeg's reason for not desiring to return to his native home, for:—"He was fearful Christianity, or rather Christians, had unfitted him for ascending the pure and undefiled throne of thirty pagan Kings before him."

Queequeg also "seemed to be saying to himself . . ., 'We cannibals must help these Christians.'" Furthermore;—"thought he, 'it's a wicked world in all meridians; I'll die a pagan.'" Another comparison states:—"The practices of whalemen soon convinced him that even Christians could be both miserable and wicked; infinitely more so than all his father's heathens."

But Melville did not countenance idolatry. He merely respected the simple religious instinct that Queequeg personified; for he said;—"Queequeg, do you see, was a creature in the transition state— neither caterpillar nor butterfly," which suggests the idea of evolution in religion. And Melville also said;—"Heaven have mercy on us all— Presbyterians and Pagans alike—for we are all somehow dreadfully cracked about the head, and sadly need mending,"—which is a stricture on all ceremonial forms of worship.

The second harpooner, Tashtego, personified *Sin*, as may be seen in the following lines;—"To look at the tawny brawn of his lithe, snaky limbs, you would almost have credited the superstitions of some of the earlier Puritans, and half believed this wild Indian to be a son of the Prince of the Powers of the Air." Moreover, the few speaking parts given to Tashtego, are blasphemous; for example;—"Stop that thunder! We don't want thunder; we want rum." And; "I say, pull like god-dam."

Third among the harpooners is Daggoo, a gigantic, coal-black negro-savage, who personified *Ignorance*. "Daggoo retained all his barbaric virtues." He was also told that his "race is the undeniable dark side of mankind."

Now it should be noted, that *Religion, Sin,* and *Ignorance,* are fundamental qualities, and that they all were personified by aborigines; and, furthermore, that Queequeg, who personified *Religion*, served Starbuck, who personified *Platonism;* and Tashtego, who personified *Sin*, served Stubb, who personified *Epicureanism;* and also that Daggoo, who personified *Ignorance*, served Flask, who personified *Stoicism,*—all of the associations being appropriate and strictly in character.

Captain Bildad, significantly named for one of Job's equivocal friends, personified *Hypocrisy*. In his last-minute admonitions to the crew, he said; —" 'Don't forget your prayers. . . . Don't whale it too much a' Lord's Day, men; but don't miss a fair chance either, that's rejecting Heaven's good gifts.' "

Captain Peleg's opinion of Captain Bildad, was expressed when he cried;—" 'Out of the cabin, ye canting, drab-colored son of a wooden gun—a straight wake with ye.' " But the most flagrant exhibition of hypocrisy was given when Captain Bildad endeavored to cheat Ishmael with an unfair "lay," and to read his Bible at the same time.

He might have succeeded, had it not been for Captain Peleg, the literal meaning of whose name is *division*, and who personified *Honesty* insisting that Ishmael should be put down for a fair share of the prospective profits. " 'Blast ye, Captain Bildad' " he said; " 'If I had followed thy advice in these matters, I would afore now had a conscience to lug about that would be heavy enough to founder the largest ship that ever sailed around Cape Horn.' "

Another character, Captain Bildad's sister, personified *Charity*. This personification is hidden by its "blinding palpableness," for; "Never did any woman better deserve her name, which was Charity —Aunt Charity, as everybody called her. And like a sister of charity—did this charitable Aunt Charity bustle about hither and thither."

With *Charity* personified so unmistakably, it is reasonable to suspect that her two associates, *Faith* and *Hope* may be found somewhere in this puzzle of words,—and so they may.

Hope is symbolized by the allegorical picture in the whalemen's Chapel, the wall of which "was adorned with a large painting representing a gallant ship beating against a terrible storm off a lee coast of black rock and snowy breakers. But high above the flying scud and dark rolling clouds, there floated a little isle of sunlight, from which beamed forth an angel's face; and this bright face shed a distinct spot of radiance upon the ship's tossed deck—'Ah noble ship,' the angel seemed to say, 'Beat on, beat on, thou noble ship, and bear a hardy helm; for lo, the sun is breaking through; the clouds are rolling off—serenest azure is at hand.' " The desperate condition of the world, symbolized by the storm-driven ship, is mitigated by a ray of hope for peace hereafter.

Faith lacks the optimistic note of the preceding belief, for its symbol is suggested by the answer to the question;—"How is it that we still refuse to be comforted for those who we nevertheless maintain are dwelling in unspeakable bliss?" And the answer is;—"Faith, like a jackal, feeds among the tombs, and even from these dead doubts, she gathers her most vital hope."

The first among the sailors, to consider, is Ishmael. This name is perfectly suited to its double meaning, for, in the superficial narrative, it is a fit name for a morbid man, who thinks that every man's hand is against him; but, as a personification, the Swedenborgian definition of the name, explains its hidden significance, which is;—The *Spiritual* and *Rational Man.*

Bulkington personified *Reason.* This character was introduced at the "Spouter-Inn." The crew of the *Grampus* had just returned from a three years' voyage, and the men went straight to the bar.

"The liquor soon mounted to their heads, as it generally does even with arrantest topers newly landed from the sea, and they began capering about most obstreperously.

"I observed, however, that one of them held somewhat aloof, and though he seemed desirous not to spoil the hilarity of his shipmates, by reason of his own sober face, yet upon the whole, he refrained from making as much noise as the rest. This man interested me at once; and since the sea-gods had ordained that he should soon become my shipmate (though but a sleeping-partner one, so far as this narrative is concerned,) I will here venture upon a little description of him.

"He stood full six feet in height, with noble shoulders, and a chest like a coffer-dam. I have seldom seen such brawn in a man . . . while in the deep shadows of his eyes, floated some reminiscences that did not seem to give him much joy.

. . . When the revelry of his companions had mounted to its height, this man slipped away unobserved. . . . In a few minutes, however, he was missed by his shipmates, and being, it seems, for some reason, a huge favourite with them, they raised a cry of 'Bulkington! Bulkington! where's Bulkington?' and darted out of the house in pursuit of him."

The allegory which is hidden in the foregoing paragraph, may be seen in the heroic figure that *Reason* requires for its personification; also, in the lines implying that reason exerts a restraining or moderating influence, with regard to excesses; and the sad "reminiscences" refer to the disappointing results of reason.

When the sailors became thoroughly drunk, *Reason* disappeared entirely, and the party ran out of the house to recover their reason in the cold air. Moreover, the parenthetical remark, to the effect that Bulkington should be but a sleeping-partner-shipmate, so far as this narrative is concerned; means that *Reason* would have no part in the fantastic, allegorical adventure.

The allegory of *Reason* is continued in the chapter entitled; "The Lee Shore." The most casual reader cannot escape the sense that this chapter deals entirely with abstractions, and that it contains some very obscure lines. But if the word *reason* is substituted for the name "Bulkington," the hidden meaning of the text will become clear. The entire chapter is here presented.

"Some chapters back, one Bulkington was spoken of, a tall, new-landed mariner, encountered in New Bedford, at the inn.

"When on that shivering winter's night, the *Pequod* thrust her vindictive bows into the cold malicious waves, who should I see standing at her helm but Bulkington. I looked with sympathetic awe and fearfulness upon the man, who in midwinter, just landed from a four years' [the change in years is in the text] voyage, could so unrestingly push off again for still another tempestuous term. The land seemed scorching to his feet. Wonderfullest things are ever the unmentionable; deep memories yield no epitaphs; this six-inch chapter is the stoneless grave of Bulkington. Let me only say that it fared with him as with the storm-tossed ship, that miserably drives along the leeward land. The port would fain give succor; the port is pitiful; in the port is safety, comfort, hearthstone, supper, warm blankets, friends, all that's kind to our mortalities. But in that gale, the port, the land, is that ship's direst jeopardy. She must fly hospitality; one touch of land, though it but graze the keel, would make her shudder through and through. With all her might she crowds all sail off shore; in so doing, fights against the very winds that fain would blow her homeward; seeks all the lashed sea's landlessness again; for refuge's sake forlornly rushing into peril; her only friend her bitterest enemy.

"Know ye now Bulkington? Glimpses do ye seem to see of that mortally intolerable truth, that all deep, earnest thinking is but the intrepid effort of the soul to keep the open independence of her sea; while the wildest winds of heaven and earth conspire to cast her on the treacherous, slavish shore?

"But as in landlessness alone resides the highest truth, shoreless, indefinite as God—so, better it is to perish in that howling infinite, than be ingloriously dashed upon the lee, even if that were safety. For worm-like, then, oh who would craven crawl to land. Terrors of the terrible, is all this agony so vain? Take heart, take heart, O Bulkington! Bear thee grimly demigod. Up from the spray of thy ocean perishing—straight up, leaps thy apotheosis."

The analogy between a storm-tossed ship, striving to keep off the rocks; and a man's reason struggling to keep clear of falsehood and dogmatism, is unmistakable; and a hint is given of Melville's poor opinion of a mind that would give up the fight, and, for the sake of spiritual ease and comfort, take shelter in the *Port of Authority*.*

The sentence;—"the land seemed scorching to his feet," is complementary to the sentence;—"in

* Note 7.

landlessness alone resides the highest truth,"—
therefore, *Reason* must keep to the open sea.

The fact that Bulkington stood at the helm of
the ship, signifies that *the world is guided by reason.*

The direct question to the reader;—"Know ye,
now, Bulkington?" is very pertinent, for it indi-
rectly informs the reader that an allegorical meaning is hidden in that character.

The final, obscure sentence;—"Up from the
spray of thy ocean perishing—straight up, leaps
thy apotheosis," will be definitely explained.

The subjects cogitated by Melville, are beyond
the reach of reason; therefore, he considered reason to be a limiting faculty. He evidently thought
that knowledge of the Infinite could be attained
only through intuition, that is, by direct cognition,
if the cumbersome cogs of reason were once destroyed by insanity.

Therefore he attached the highest importance to
the spiritual power; *Intuition;* and for its personification, he utilized "the most mournful, perchance
the most abased among them all"; for, he allotted
that character to Pip, the little black boy from
Alabama.

After Pip lost his mind, through fright, when he
jumped out of the whale boat, Melville touched
"that workman's arm with some ethereal light";

and "spread a rainbow over his disastrous set of sun," in the following manner.

"The sea had jeeringly kept his finite body up, but drowned the infinite of his soul. Not drowned entirely though. Rather carried down alive to wondrous depths, where . . . Wisdom revealed his hoarded heaps . . . and ever juvenile eternities. He saw God's foot upon the treadle of the loom, and spoke it; and therefore his shipmates called him mad. So man's insanity is heaven's sense; and wandering from all mortal reason, man comes at last to that celestial thought, which, to reason, is absurd and frantic."

Insanity is glorified further, when Pip lifted "himself to the exalted mounts," by saying, to the supposedly dying Queequeg; "Poor rover, will ye never have done with all this weary roving? Where go ye now? But if currents carry ye to those sweet Antilles, where the beaches are only beat with water-lilies, will ye do one little errand for me? Seek out one Pip, who's now been missing long; I think he's in those far Antilles. If ye find him, then comfort him."

Starbuck, who overheard Pip, reasoned thus;—

"I have heard . . . that in violent fevers, men all ignorance, have talked in ancient tongues; and that when the mystery is probed, it turns out always that in their wholly forgotten childhood, those ancient tongues had been really spoken in their hearing by some lofty scholars. So, to my fond faith, poor Pip, in this strange sweetness of his lunacy, brings heavenly vouchers of all our heavenly homes, where learned he that but there?"

Another tribute was paid to *Intuition*, by Captain Ahab, when he said;—"Now, then, Pip, we'll talk this over; I do suck most wondrous philosophies from thee. Some unknown conduits from the unknown worlds must empty into thee." And again, when Pip was seized by a sailor, Captain Ahab ordered; "Hands off that holiness." Also when Pip took his turn at reading the symbols on the doubloon, he was the only one who saw their real significance, for he said;—" 'When aught's nailed to the mast, it's a sign that things grow desperate. Ha, ha, old Ahab, the White Whale; he'll nail ye. . . . Oh, the gold, the precious gold, the green miser'll hoard ye soon.' "

The substitution of intuition for reason, explains the obscure line regarding Bulkington;—"Up from the spray of thy ocean-perishing—straight up, leaps thy apotheosis," for it means, according to Melville, that reason, when destroyed, is replaced with celestial understanding.

Another personification of an abstraction, is found in the old Manx sailor, for he represented *Prescience*. "The old sea traditions invested this old Manxman with preternatural powers of discernment."

When he, in turn, read the symbols on the doubloon, he gave the following interpretation:—

" 'If the White Whale be raised, it must be in a month and a day, when the sun stands in some one of those signs. . . . Now, in what sign will the sun then be? The horseshoe sign,—for there it is, right opposite the gold. [A horseshoe was nailed to the opposite side of the mast.] And what's the horseshoe sign? The lion is the horseshoe sign— the roaring and devouring lion. Ship, old ship, my old head shakes to think of thee.' "

When the ship *Rachael* hove in sight, and before a word had been exchanged with her, the old Manxman muttered;—" 'Bad news, she brings bad news.' " He also declared, with reference to the unknown fate of the son of the *Rachael's* captain: " 'He's drowned with the rest on 'em last night.' " And shortly before the catastrophe, he felt the approaching calamity, for he remarked:—" 'The skewer seems loosening out of the middle of the world.' "

The ship carpenter personified the practical virtue, *Art,* combining *Originality* and *Inventiveness.* More than two pages are devoted to the analysis of this character, beginning with:—

"Seat thyself sultanically among the moons of Saturn, and take high abstracted man alone, and he seems a wonder, a grandeur, and a woe. But from the same point take mankind in mass, and for the most part they seem a mob of unnecessary duplicates, both contemporary and hereditary. But most humble though he was, and far from furnishing an example of the high, humane abstraction, the *Pequod's* carpenter was no duplicate; hence, he now comes in person on this stage. . . . He was, to a certain off-handed, practical extent, alike experienced in numerous trades and callings. . . . This carpenter of the *Pequod* was singularly efficient in those thousand nameless mechanical emergencies continually recurring in a large ship. . . . He was a stripped abstract; and unfractioned integral; uncompromised as a new-born babe; living without premeditated reference to this world or the next. . . . He did not seem to work so by reason or by instinct, or simply because he had been tutored to it . . . but merely by a kind of deaf and dumb, spontaneous, literal process."

"Captain Ahab said to the carpenter;—'Thou art as unprincipled as the gods, and as much of a jack-of-all-trades.' "

Perth, the blacksmith, personified *Remorse,* for he had been ruined both physically and socially, through intemperance.

"He was an old man, who, at the age of nearly sixty, postponedly encountered that thing in sorrow's technicals called ruin. . . . No murmur, no impatience, no petulance did come from him. Silent, slow, and solemn; bowing over still further,

[71]

his chronically broken back, he toiled away, as if
toil were life itself, and the heavy beating of his
hammer, the heavy beating of his heart. And so
it was.—Most miserable."

The black cook, Fleece, personified *Mockery*, as
revealed by his profane sermon to the sharks.

Doughboy, the steward, personified *Cowardice*,
as shown by his cringing behavior on all occasions,
"Doughboy's life was one continual lip-quiver."

Fedallah personified the *Future*. This character
is scarcely given material existence, even in the superficial story, for he is referred to repeatedly, as a
shadow, and a phantom, and "that hair-turbaned
Fedallah remained a muffled mystery to the last.
. . . He was such a creature as civilized, domestic
people, in the temperate zone, only see in their
dreams, and that but dimly."

Elijah, in the chapter entitled; "The Prophet,"
saw the *Future*, in the person of Fedallah, through
the fog; "very dim, very dim." Fedallah was, on
board the ship, hidden from the inhabitants of the
symbolical world, and the mysterious sounds which
came from his hiding place, symbolized *Omens*
and *Portents*. And when Fedallah "was calmly
eyeing the right whale's head, and ever and anon
glancing from the deep wrinkles there, to the lines
in his own hand," he was identifying himself with
the future, and moreover, he interpreted Ahab's
dream of impending doom.

The crew, collectively, of the symbolical ship,

[72]

represented the entire human race; for they were gathered from "all the isles of the sea, and all the ends of the earth."

Every spoken word is a symbol of the emotion that gave it utterance, and so the lines spoken by the sailor-actors, in the allegorical play, which was staged on the forecastle, symbolize the virtues, vices, passions, and other qualities of mind and heart. The emotions which are common to all mankind, are spoken in chorus, and the meanings of the somewhat queer conversation are here given in the order in which they were spoken.

All	Love
1st Nantucket sailor	Duty
Mate's voice	Authority
2nd Nantucket sailor	Obedience
Dutch sailor	Thoroughness
French sailor	Initiative
Pip	Indifference
French sailor	Joy
Iceland sailor	Sorrow
Maltese sailor	Imagination
Sicilian sailor	Frivolity
Long Island sailor	Thrift
Azore sailor	Enthusiasm
Pip	Destructiveness
China sailor	Fantasy
French sailor	Ecstasy
Tashtego	Apathy
Old Manx sailor	Grief
3rd Nantucket sailor	Excess

Lascar sailor	Foresight
Maltese sailor	Passion
Sicilian sailor	Continence
Tahitian sailor	Patriotism
Portuguese sailor	Observation
Danish sailor	Confidence
4th Nantucket sailor . . .	Boldness
English sailor	Loyalty
All	Self-esteem
Old Manx sailor	Foreboding
Daggoo	Superstition
Spanish sailor	Spitefulness
Daggoo	Forbearance
St. Jago's sailor	Speculation
5th Nantucket sailor . . .	Inquisitiveness
Spanish sailor	Malice
Daggoo	Anger
Spanish sailor	Quarrelsomeness
All	Excitement
Tashtego	Blasphemy
Belfast sailor	Strife
English sailor	Justice
Old Manx sailor	Judgement
Mate's voice	Prudence
All	Self-preservation
Pip	Fear*

Repentance is symbolized by a tear, according to the following excerpt;—

"The lovely aroma in that enchanted air did at

* See analysis of the Allegorical Play.

last seem to dispel, for a moment, the cankerous thing in his (Ahab's) soul. That glad, happy air, that winsome sky, did at last stroke and caress him; the stepmother world, so long cruel—forbidding— now threw affectionate arms around his stubborn neck, and did seem to joyously sob over him, as if over one, that however wilful and erring, she could yet find it in her heart to save and to bless. From beneath his slouched hat, Ahab dropped a tear into the sea; nor did all the Pacific contain such wealth as that wee drop."

It is an interesting coincidence, that the Peri, in *Lallah Rookh*, gained admission to Paradise, with a tear of repentance, after the most precious things of earth had been rejected.

The *will to believe* is presented twice, by Star-buck, the Platonist. The occasion is found at the end of his reading of the doubloon symbols, when he said;—"I will quit it, lest Truth shake me falsely." And the second time, when "gazing far down from his boat's side into that same golden sea," [that is, meditating upon life] he "lowly murmured;—'Loveliness unfathomable as ever lover saw in his young bride's eye!—Tell me not of thy teeth-tiered sharks, and thy kidnapping cannibal ways. Let faith oust fact; let fancy oust memory; I look deep down and do believe.' "

VII

MELVILLE often made use of the analogy between actual travel on this earth, and intellectual excursions into the realm of mysticism. His method was to keep the two ideas parallel; for whatever may be said of the one, will apply with equal meaning to the other. The circumnavigation of the physical globe, by a whaling ship; was paralleled by the circumnavigation of the wonder world in his mind.

The following paragraph gives an example of the transition from the description of physical travel, to that of metaphysical exploration;—

"Were this world an endless plain, and by sailing eastward we could forever reach new distances, and discover sights more sweet and strange than any Cyclades or Islands of King Solomon, then there were promise in the voyage. But in pursuit of those far mysteries we dream of, or in tormented chase of that demon phantom, that, some time or other, swims before all human hearts—while chasing such over this round globe, they either lead us on in barren mazes, or midway leave us whelmed."

The same analogy is elaborated, and the circular routine of spiritual progress is described in detail, as follows:—

"There is no steady unretracing progress in this

life; we do not advance through fixed gradations, and at the last one pause;—through infancy's unconscious spell, boyhood's thoughtless faith, adolescence, doubt, (the common doom,) then scepticism, then disbelief, resting at last in manhood's pondering repose of If. But once gone through, we trace the round again; and are infants, boys, and men, and Ifs eternally."

In the light of the foregoing excerpts, a hidden meaning, suggesting the futility of speculating upon the unknowable, may be seen in Melville's query:—"But whereto does all that circumnavigation conduct? Only through numberless perils to the point whence we started, where those that we left behind secure, were all the time before us."

This same intellectual experience; reasoning in a circle, or following a labyrinthine line of thought, and finally returning to the starting point, is presented in parable form in the chapter entitled;—"A Bower in the Arsacides." This chapter describes a whale's skeleton that was worshiped as a god, by the natives, and, Ishmael, assuming it to be a symbol of the Deity, relates:—

"To and fro I paced before this skeleton . . . and with a ball of Arsacidean twine, wandered, eddied long amid its many windings, shaded colonnades and arbours. But soon my line was out; and following it back, I emerged from the opening where I entered."

The complication of obstacles encountered, and the need of a line with which to explore an object of less than one hundred feet in length, are enough to notify the reader that "it has the savour of analogical probability."

The experience of Melville was the same as that of Omar Khyyam, for, the old Persian poet, centuries ago, concerning metaphysical speculation, wrote:—

"Myself when young did eagerly frequent
Doctor and Saint, and heard great argument
About it and about; but evermore
Came out by the same door where in I went."*

One of the most effective lines with a double meaning, is the declaration;—"I am tormented with an everlasting itch for things remote. I love to sail forbidden seas and land on barbarous coasts."

The analogy which these lines contain, is distinctly pointed out in another paragraph, which describes a forbidden sea, and warns against the danger of embarking thereon,—

"Consider all this; and then turn to this green, gentle and most docile earth; consider them both, the sea and the land; and do you not find a strange analogy to something in yourself? For as this appalling ocean surrounds the verdant land, so in

* Rubaiyat of Omar Khayyam.

the soul of man there lies one insular Tahiti, full of peace and joy, but encompassed by all the horrors of the half-known life. God keep thee. Push not off from that isle, thou cans't never return."

It is hardly necessary to point out that the preceding paragraph advises against the abandonment of a comfortable, simple faith, in exchange for the mental anguish of speculation and doubt; for it is an unconcealed example of the parallelism of Melville's method, and explains itself.

Taking up the symbols again, we find that there is an important one, upon which Melville devoted considerable space; and that one is *water;* for it is the symbol of *Truth.* This symbol is silent; but its meaning may be readily discovered in the following paragraph;—

"Let the most absent-minded of men be plunged in his deepest reveries—stand that man on his legs, set his feet a-going, and he will infallibly lead you to water, if water there be in all that region. Should you ever be athirst in the great American desert, try this experiment, if your caravan happen to be supplied with a metaphysical professor. Yes, as every one knows, meditation and water (truth) are wedded forever."

Another important symbol is the *sea,* for it is the symbol of *Life.* To Melville, the sea was a living symbol, which strengthens its analogy to life, for; when off the Cape of Good Hope, he added to his musings;—"And heaved, and heaved, still unrestingly heaved the black sea, as if its vast tides were a conscience, and the great mundane soul were in anguish and remorse for the long sin and suffering it has bred." And again;—"Thus this mysterious divine Pacific zones the world's whole bulk about; makes all coasts one bay to it; seems the tide-beating heart of earth."

The man at the masthead also "takes the mystic ocean at his feet for the visible image of that deep, blue, bottomless soul, pervading mankind and nature." Another analogy to life is given in the words;—"The robust and man-like sea heaved with long, strong, lingering swells, as Samson's chest in his sleep." And again;—"There is one knows not what sweet mystery about this sea, whose gently awful stirrings seem to speak of some hidden soul beneath."

A closer analogy to life occurs in the line;— "Yet not a modern sun ever sets, but in precisely the same manner, the live sea swallows up ships and crews."* Another line to the same effect, is; —"That unsounded ocean you gasp in, is Life; those sharks, your foes; those spades, your friends; and what between sharks and spades, you are in a sad pickle and peril poor lad."

This is pure symbolism. The ocean has been sounded, but life has not; and the predicament in

* Note 3.

which a man might find himself, between his friends and his enemies, is a cynical comment upon Melville's own personal experience.

Melville gives the reader a few rather shrewd hints, in the beginning of the book, concerning the subject matter, for, when after commenting upon the holy awe in which the ancients held the sea, he concludes;—

"Surely all this is not without meaning. And still deeper the meaning of that story of Narcissus, who because he could not grasp the tormenting, mild image he saw in the fountain, plunged into it and was drowned. But that same image, we ourselves see in all rivers and oceans. It is the image of the ungraspable phantom of life; and that is the key to it all." The phrase;—"key to it all," applies to what is to follow, as well as to what has been already stated.

The same deep meaning which Melville found hidden in the story of Narcissus, is again hidden by Melville, in the lines:—"Slowly crossing the deck from the scuttle, Ahab leaned over the side, and watched how his shadow in the water sank and sank to his gaze, the more and the more that he strove to pierce the profundity,"—signifying, of course, *the elusiveness of the meaning of life.*

With these two symbols understood, namely, *water,* as the symbol of *Truth,* and the *ocean* as the symbol of *Life,* the allegorical analogy in the following lines, may be separated from the literal meaning of the text.

"If they but knew it, almost all men in their degree, some time or other, cherish very nearly the same feelings towards the ocean with me. . . . Look at the crowds of water-gazers there. Circumambulate the city on a dreamy Sabbath afternoon. . . . What do you see?—Posted like silent sentinels all around the town, stand thousands upon thousands of mortal men fixed in ocean reveries. Some leaning against the spiles; some seated upon the pier-heads; some looking over the bulwarks of ships from China; some high aloft in the rigging, as if striving to get a still better sea-ward peep. . . . But look, here come more crowds pacing straight for the water. . . . They must get just as nigh the water as they possibly can without falling in. And there they stand—miles of them —leagues. Inlanders all, they come from lanes and alleys, streets and avenues—north, east, south, and west. Yet here they all unite."

The extravagance of the last lines is ample evidence that Melville's description does not apply to real life; for the bizarre picture presented is rather mystifying, if taken literally, and visualized; but as a parable it will pass.

The "thousands upon thousands of mortal men fixed in ocean reveries," represent the universal interest felt by mankind, in the problem of life. The "water-gazers," otherwise, *truth-seekers*, are shown "in their degree" (of intelligence,) by "some leaning against the spiles," who are representative of the lowest intellectual level; "some seated upon the pier-heads," who personify a higher degree of intelligence; while, "some looking over the bulwarks of ships from China," refers to the scholars who turn to Oriental philosophies for the truth. Those who are "high aloft in the rigging, as if striving to get a still better sea-ward peep," represent the highest intellects, which, of course, see the farthest. Moreover, "In landlessness alone, resides the highest truth." It should be noted that all of the foregoing spectacle may be seen on "a dreamy Sabbath afternoon," which is very fitting, for it is an appropriate time for men to ponder life and destiny.

Having learned through Melville's analogies, that almost all mankind are, more or less, occupied with thoughts of whither and wherefore, we may take up the first parable, or hidden allegory.

This allegory, which is somewhat reminiscent of *Pilgrim's Progress*, begins with a confession, which, under the similitude of worldly experience, describes the spiritual experience of the *rational man*, who, depressed by thoughts on the futility of life, and the uncertainty of the hereafter, sets out to find spiritual rest and comfort, instead of resorting to "Pistol and ball."

In his first adventure, a certain type of religion is investigated, as appears in the following excerpt.

"But presently I came to a smoky light proceeding from a low, wide building, the door of which stood invitingly open. It had a careless look, as if meant for the uses of the public; so, entering, the first thing I did, was to stumble over an ashbox in the porch. 'Ha,' thought I, 'Ha,' as the flying particles choked me, 'Are these the ashes from that destroyed city Gomorrah?' But 'The Crossed Harpoons' and 'The Sword Fish'? this, then must needs be the sign of 'The Trap.'

"However I picked myself up, and hearing a loud voice within, pushed on and opened a second door. It seemed the Great Black Parliament sitting in Tophet. A hundred black faces turned in their rows to peer; and beyond, a black Angel of Doom was beating a book in a pulpit. It was a negro church; and the preacher's text was about the blackness of darkness and the weeping and wailing and teeth-gnashing there. 'Ha, Ishmael,' muttered I, backing out, 'Wretched entertainment at the sign of 'The Trap.'"

The symbols of hell and punishment are so plentiful here, that it would be superfluous to name them; but the meaning is, to show the rational man's contempt for a religion which is based upon terror. He considered *fear* to be a crude expedient to entice people to seek the protection of religion, for, it is significant that twice, for emphasis, he called the *church*, "*The Trap*."

Moreover, the "smoky light," is the symbol of the *dull spiritual light* that could invent and preach such a doctrine, while the color of the congregation symbolizes the low intelligence of its followers. This interpretation is consistent with the allegorical character of Daggoo, the African harpooner, who personified *Ignorance*, and ignorance is the parent of fear.

Melville also stated openly, his aversion to the element, fear, in religion, when he said;—

"I have no objection to any person's religion, be it what it may, so long as that person does not kill or insult any other person, because that other person don't believe it also. But when a man's religion becomes really frantic; when it is a positive torment to him; and, in fine, makes this earth of ours an uncomfortable inn to lodge in; then I think it high time to take that individual aside and argue the point with him."

Again, speaking through Captain Peleg, he said; —"Fiery pit; fiery pit; ye insult me, man, past all natural bearing, ye insult me. It's an all-fired outrage to tell any human creature that he's bound to hell."

After leaving "The Trap," Ishmael, the rational man, arrived at the "Spouter-Inn," and when he saw the sign bearing the words; "Spouter-Inn,—

Peter Coffin," he remarked;—"Coffin?—Spouter? Rather ominous in that particular connection."

The significance of the connection, which Ishmael saw, was in the symbolical meaning of the sign. "Spouter," is a localism for the whale; and the *Whale* is the symbol of *Fate*. "Inn" is a symbol of the *earth*, and was so used by Melville in the last paragraph quoted, while "*coffin*," is "the very dreaded symbol of grim death." Naturally, Ishmael was shocked to be reminded of the intimate relation of *Fate* and *Death* with the *World*.

A covert hint is given, touching the analogy between the inn and the earth, in the line;—"The dilapidated little wooden house itself looked as if it might have been carted from some burnt district." Now, as the earth, itself, is believed to have come from some burnt district, the analogy is very obvious. Moreover, Melville combined the inn-world symbol with the ship-world symbol, when he described the "old fashioned wainscots, reminding one of the bulwarks of some condemned old craft." The analogy is carried further, in the words;—"It stood on a sharp, bleak corner, where that tempestuous wind, Euroclydon kept up a worse howling than it did about St. Paul's tossed craft."

The analogy between the world, and a ship in a storm, occurs repeatedly, and the adversities which beset mankind on earth, are referred to, as;—"this life's howling gale."

Another allegory, relating to the hidden theme of the book, is given in the description of a "boggy, soggy, squitchy picture," that hung on the wall in the "Spouter-Inn." Considerable space is taken up to impress upon the reader, the obscurity and mystery of the subject. Ishmael's conclusion, as to the meaning of the picture, is as follows;—

"In fact the artist's design seemed this; a final theory of my own, partly based upon the aggregated opinions of many aged persons with whom I conversed upon the subject. The picture represents a Cape Horner in a great hurricane; the half-foundered ship weltering there with its three dismantled masts alone visible; and an exasperated whale, purposing to spring clean over the craft, is in the enormous act of impaling himself upon the three mastheads."

This is a symbolical picture of Melville's conception of a suffering world, dominated by a malignant Fate, according to the design of the artist, —meaning the Creator. The aggregated opinions of many aged persons with whom he conversed upon the subject, means the conclusion he had reached, as a result of his philosophical and metaphysical studies.

VIII

ISHMAEL, in his search for spiritual rest, found that the only bed available, at the "Spouter-Inn" or *Fated-world*, was the bed of Queequeg, the cannibal harpooner, who personified *Religion*. Ishmael wavered in his choice between the soft bed of religion, and the hard bench of philosophy, as follows:

" 'Landlord, I've changed my mind about that harpooner,—I shan't sleep with him, I'll try the bench here!' 'Just as you please; I'm sorry I can't spare ye a table-cloth for a mattress, and it's a plaguy rough board here'—feeling of the knots and notches. 'But wait a bit, Skrimshander; I've got a carpenter's plane there in the bar—wait, I say, and I'll make ye snug enough.' So saying, he procured the plane; and with his old silk handker-chief, first dusting the bench, vigorously set to planing away at my bed, the while grinning like an ape. The shavings flew right and left; till at last the plane came bump against a indestructible knot. The landlord was near spraining his wrist, and I told him for heaven's sake to quit."

The signs of hidden meanings here, are in the absurdity of planing a wooden bench to make it comfortable to sleep upon, and in the unnecessary operation of first dusting it. Moreover, the whimsical regret of the landlord, regarding a table cloth for a mattress, serves to forestall the reader's question concerning bed-clothes, which would be the first thing to be considered under such circumstances.

The interpretation is, that the rational man first decided to seek consolation in philosophy, and secured a volume, which, after it was dusted with the old silk handkerchief, he proceeded to read. He turned page after page, which are represented by the shavings flying right and left, and was making satisfactory progress, until the *plane of logic* struck a knotty problem which it could not smooth away. The parable continues:—

"I now took the measure of the bench, and found that it was a foot too short; but that could be mended with a chair. But it was a foot too narrow, and the other bench in the room was about four inches higher than the planed one—so there was no yoking them."

This means; that as the first system of philosophy did not meet his requirements, he endeavored to combine other systems with it; but they could not be harmonized. Finally, he decided to accept the bed of religion, and said;—"I tumbled into bed, and commended myself to heaven . . . and never slept better in my life," all of which goes to show the easy comfort of religion,—a matter of faith, and the shifting of responsibility, in comparison with the hard requirements of philosophy,—a matter of reason and self-reliance.

The allegory or parable is continued further, and describes another aspect of religion;—

"Upon waking next morning about daylight, I found Queequeg's arm thrown over me in the most loving manner, you had almost thought I had been his wife. The counterpane was of patch work, full of little parti-colored squares and triangles; and this arm of his, tattooed all over with an interminable Cretan labyrinth of a figure, no two parts of which were of one precise shade,—this same arm of his, I say, looked for all the world like a strip of that same quilt. Indeed, partly lying on it, as the arm did, when I first awoke, I could hardly tell it from the quilt, they so blended their hues together. . . . My sensations were strange. Let me try to explain them."

The implication here is; that religion, although a comfort to mankind, is, nevertheless, on account of its many forms and creeds, a fabrication of variegated patchwork.

The words;—"My sensations were strange. Let me try to explain them," are followed by a page, descriptive of a boyhood experience, of which the following is the climax;—

"Instantly I felt a shock running through my whole frame; nothing was to be seen, and nothing was to be heard; but a supernatural hand seemed placed in mine . . . and for days and weeks and months afterwards, I lost myself in confounding attempts to explain the mystery. Nay, to this very hour, I often puzzle myself with it. . . . My sensations at feeling the supernatural hand in mine, were very similar, in their strangeness, to those which I experienced on waking up and seeing Queequeg's pagan arm thrown round me."

This wierd passage means that when a man accepts religion, he faces a mystery, and he also feels that he is led by a supernatural hand. The reference to married life, suggests the idea of embracing religion, or being united with the Church.

In another paragraph, Melville sees the Bible symbolized by Queequeg's tattooing, for;—

"This tattooing had been the work of a departed prophet and seer of his island, who by those hieroglyphic marks, had written out on his body a complete theory of the heavens and the earth, and a mystical treatise on the art of attaining truth; so that Queequeg, in his own proper person, was a riddle to unfold; a wondrous work in one volume; but whose mysteries not even himself could read, though his own live heart beat against them; and these mysteries were therefore destined in the end to moulder away with the living parchment whereon they were inscribed, and so be unsolved to the last. And this thought it must have been which suggested to Ahab that wild exclamation of his, when

[91]

one morning turning away from surveying poor Queequeg,—'O! devilish tantalization of the gods!'"

The analogy between Queequeg's tattooing and the Bible, is very close. The books of Moses and the prophets, as well as the New Testament, are suggested; it is also a wondrous work in one volume; and a hint is given, that religion, itself, though its life depends upon it, does not understand the Bible. Moreover, Melville considers the Bible to be a riddle to unfold, and the perplexing obscurity of divine revelation, accounts for Ahab's exasperation.

Another instance of Queequeg's tattooing symbolizing the Bible, may be seen when Queequeg read the symbols on the doubloon. On this doubloon, mountains were represented, which may be considered as symbolical of the earth; and on it, also, were the signs of the zodiac, symbolical of the heavens. Therefore, when Queequeg, who personified *Religion,* undertook to disclose the meaning of the universe, which was symbolized by the doubloon, he turned to his tattooing, which was symbolical of the Bible.

Stubb, who had been listening to the various interpretations, remarked, upon the approach of Queequeg;—

". . . Here comes Queequeg—all tattooing—looks like the signs of the zodiac himself. What says the cannibal? As I live, he's comparing notes; looking at his thigh bone; thinks the sun is in the thigh, or in the calf, or in the bowels, I suppose, as the old women talk Surgeon's Astronomy in the back country. And by Jove, he's found something there in the vicinity of his thigh,—I guess it's Sagittarius, or the Archer. No; he don't know what to make of the doubloon." This implies the futility of searching the Scriptures for the meaning of the universe.

Melville's scepticism regarding the Divine inspiration of the Bible, may be found in the words of Ahab;—"If the gods think to speak outright to man, they will honourably speak outright; not shake their heads and give an old wife's darkling hint."

Evidently, Melville felt that the power manifested in the universe, is fundamentally cruel, and is without justice or mercy. A hint of this attitude is given in Father Mapple's sermon, which ends with;—"O! Father—chiefly known by Thy rod." Melville also complained of "the demonism in the world," and "the horrible vulturism of earth"; and he also asks the question; "Cannibals? Who is not a cannibal?" With more directness, he asserts;

"There can be no hearts above the snow line. . . . Look, see yon albicore, who put it into him to chase and fang yon flying-fish? Where do murderers go? Who's to doom when the judge himself is dragged to the bar?" In another line, we have; "Lo! ye believers in gods all goodness, and in man all ill, lo! you, see the omniscient gods oblivious of suffering man; and man, though idiotic, and knowing not what he does, yet full of the sweet things of love and gratitude." Furthermore, a very caustic inuendo is hidden in an observation, made after a survey of the whale's head;

"In phrenological phrase you would say—This man had no self-esteem, and no veneration. And by those negations, considered along with the affirmative fact of this prodigious bulk and power, you can best form to yourself the truest, though not the most exhilarating conception of what the most exalted potency is."

IX

THROUGHOUT the book, Melville interpolated allusions to passages in the Scriptures. Some are stated plainly; but other ones are carefully concealed. The first one is comparatively clear;—"What of it?" he asks, "If some old hunks of a sea-captain orders me to get a broom and sweep down the decks? What does that indignity amount to, weighed, I mean, in the scales of the New Testament?" The answer is:—*"Servants, be obedient to them that are your masters according to the flesh, with fear and trembling, in singleness of heart."**

Another example, admittedly obscure, is hidden in the words;—"Not ignoring what is good, I am quick to perceive a horror, and could still be sociable with it—would they let me—since it is but well to be on friendly terms with all the inmates of the place one lodges in." This means *"Love your enemies."*†

The precept;—*"Lay not up for yourselves treasures upon earth,"*‡ is presented openly, in the discussion concerning Ishmael's share in the profits of the proposed voyage.

---

* Ephesians, 6, 5.
† Luke, 6, 27.
‡ Matthew, 6, 19.

Another Scriptural teaching is alluded to when Melville pondered the symbolical meaning of ambergris:—"Now that the incorruption of this most fragrant ambergris should be found in the heart of such decay; is this nothing? Bethink ye of that saying of St. Paul, in Corinthians, about corruption and incorruption; how that we are sown in dishonor, but raised in glory."*

Inasmuch as Melville referred to one lesson in Corinthians, it suggests another, from the same epistle, but which is concealed. It is found in the incident, wherein Queequeg, who personified *Religion*, and who, after lying in his coffin, waiting for death, suddenly rallied and recovered his health; the meaning of which is;—"*O Grave, where is thy victory.*"† Other direct quotations are "*All is vanity*,"‡ and "*The man that wandereth out of the way of understanding shall remain in the congregation of the dead.*"§

A rather severe implication that religion is a burden to the people, is adapted from the Old Testament. It may be found in the incident which describes Queequeg, who personified *Religion*, sitting upon the prostrate form of a sleeping sailor. Ishmael remonstrated, but Queequeg replied;—

* Corinthians, 15, 43, 53.
† Corinthians, 15, 55.
‡ Ecclesiastes, 1, 2.
§ Proverbs, 21, 16.

"Won't hurt him face." Ishmael exclaimed;—
"Face, call that his face? . . . Get off, Queequeg,
you are heavy, it's *grinding the face of the poor*."*

Melville is more explicit in his opinion concerning the burden of religion, when he asks the question;

"What is the Archbishop of Savesoul's income
of 100,000 pounds, seized from the scant bread
and cheese of hundreds of thousands of broken-
back laborers; what is that globular 100,000 pounds
but a Fast-Fish?"

A curious interpretation of the Golden Rule,
which satirizes evangelism, is given when Queequeg, instead of accepting Presbyterianism, at Ishmael's solicitation, invited Ishmael to join with
him in the worship of the little, black idol, Yojo.
Ishmael pondered the question, as follows;—

"But what is worship?—to do the will of God
—that is worship. And what is the will of God?—
to do to my fellow man what I would have my fellow man do to me—that is the will of God. Now
Queequeg is my fellow man. And what do I wish
that this Queequeg would do to me? Why unite
with me in my particular Presbyterian form of
worship. Consequently I must then unite with
him in his; ergo, I must turn idolator."

One of the most involved parables is the chapter, entitled; "Queen Mab." The caption alone,

*Isaiah, 3, 15.

[97]

is a hint at the fantastical character of the subject matter. This parable conceals the proverb; *"For as a man thinketh in his heart, so is he"*;* the precept; *"It is hard for thee to kick against the pricks"*;† the doctrine of *nonresistance;* and the admonition; *"Unto him that smiteth thee on the one cheek, offer also the other."*‡ The entire chapter is here given.

"Next morning Stubb accosted Flask, 'Such a queer dream, King Post, I never had. You know the old man's ivory leg, well I dreamed he kicked me with it; and when I tried to kick back, upon my soul, my little man, I kicked my leg right off! And then, Presto! Ahab seemed a pyramid, and I, like a blazing fool, kept kicking at it. But what was still more curious, Flask—you know how curious all dreams are—through all this rage that I was in, I somehow seemed to be thinking to myself, that after all, it was not much of an insult, that kick from Ahab.' 'Why' thinks I, 'What's the row? It's not a real leg, only a false leg.' And there's a mighty difference between a living thump and a dead thump. That's what makes a blow from the hand, Flask, fifty times more savage to bear than a blow from a cane.§ The living mem-

* Proverbs, 23, 7.
† Acts, 9, 5.
‡ Luke, 6, 29.
§ Note 8.

ber—that makes the living insult, my little man.
And thinks I to myself all the while, mind, while I
was stubbing my silly toes against that cursed pyramid—so confoundedly contradictory was it all, all
the while, I say, I was thinking to myself, 'What's
his leg now, but a cane—a whalebone cane.' 'Yes,'
thinks I, 'it was only a playful cudgelling—in fact,
only a whale-boning that he gave me—not a base
kick.' 'Besides,' thinks I, 'look at it once; why, the
end of it—the foot part—what a small sort of end
it is; whereas, if a broad-footed farmer kicked me,
there's a devilish broad insult. But this insult is
whittled down to a point only.' But now comes
the greatest joke of the dream, Flask. While I
was battering away at the pyramid, a sort of badger-
haired old merman, with a hump on his back,
takes me by the shoulders, and slews me round.
'What are you 'bout?' says he. 'Slid! man, but I
was frightened. Such a phiz! But, somehow, next
moment I was over the fright. 'What am I about?'
says I at last. 'And what business is that of yours,
I should like to know, Mr. Humpback? Do *you*
want a kick?' By the lord Flask, I had no sooner
said that, than he turned round his stern to me,
bent over, and dragging a lot of seaweed he had
for a clout,—what do you think I saw?—why thunder alive, man, his stern was stuck full of marlin-
spikes, with the points out. Says I, on second
thought, 'I guess I won't kick you, old fellow,'

'Wise Stubb,' said he, 'wise Stubb'; and kept muttering it all the time, a sort of eating his own gums like a chimney hag. Seeing he wasn't going to stop saying over his 'wise Stubb, wise Stubb,' I thought I might as well fall to kicking the pyramid again. But I had only just lifted my foot for it, when he roared out, 'Stop that kicking,' 'Halloa,' says I, 'What's the matter now, old fellow?' 'Look ye here,' says he; 'let's argue the insult. Captain Ahab kicked ye, didn't he?' 'Yes, he did,' says I —'right *here* it was.' 'Very good,' says he—'he used his ivory leg, didn't he?' 'Yes, he did,' says I. 'Well then,' says he, 'wise Stubb, what have you to complain of? Didn't he kick you with a right good will? It wasn't a common pitch pine leg he kicked you with, was it? No, you were kicked by a great man, and with a beautiful ivory leg, Stubb. In old England, the greatest lords think it great glory to be slapped by a queen, and made garter-knights of; but, be *your* boast, Stubb, that ye were kicked by old Ahab, and made a wise man of. Remember what I say; *be* kicked by him; account his kicks honors; and on no account kick back; for you can't help yourself, wise Stubb. Don't you see that pyramid?' With that, he all of a sudden seemed somehow, in some queer fashion, to swim off into the air. I snored; rolled over; and there I was in my hammock. Now, what do you think of that dream, Flask?"

Another New Testament doctrine is ingeniously hidden in the following preposterous episode, of which, Melville, himself, said; "I know that this queer adventure of the Gay-Header's will be sure to seem incredible to some landsmen." It occurred while Tashtego and Daggoo were at work, dipping spermaceti from the whale's head.

"Now, the people of the *Pequod* had been bailing for some time in this way; several tubs had been filled with the fragrant sperm; when all at once, a queer accident happened. Whether it was that Tashtego, that wild Indian, was so heedless and reckless as to let go for a moment his one-handed hold on the great cabled tackles suspending the head; or whether the place where he stood was so treacherous and oozy; or whether the Evil One himself would have it to fall out so, without stating his particular reason; how it was exactly, there is no telling now; but, on a sudden, as the eightieth or ninetieth bucket came suckingly up— my god! poor Tashtego—like the twin reciprocating bucket in a veritable well, dropped head foremost down into this great Tun of Heidelburg, and with a horrible oily gurgle, went clean out of sight.

" 'Man overboard,' cried Daggoo, who amid the general consternation, first came to his senses. 'Swing the bucket this way,' and putting one foot into it, so as the better to secure his slippery handhold on the whip itself, the hoisters ran him high up to the top of the head, almost before Tashtego could have reached its interior bottom. Meantime, there was a terrific tumult. Looking over the side, they saw the before lifeless head throbbing and heaving just below the surface of the sea, as if that moment seized with some momentous idea; whereas it was only the poor Indian unconsciously revealing by those struggles, the perilous depth to which he had sunk.

"At this instant, while Daggoo, on the summit of the head, was clearing the whip—which had somehow got foul of the great cutting tackles—a sharp cracking noise was heard; and to the unspeakable horror of all, one of the two enormous hooks suspending the head tore out, and with a vast vibration, the enormous mass sideways swung, till the drunk ship reeled and shook as if smitten by an iceberg. The one remaining hook, upon which the entire strain now depended, seemed every instant to be on the point of giving way; an event still more likely from the violent motions of the head.

" 'Come down, come down,' yelled the seamen to Daggoo, but with one hand holding to the heavy tackles, so that if the head should drop, he would still remain suspended; the negro having cleared the foul line, rammed down the bucket into the now collapsed well, meaning that the buried harpooner should grasp it, and so be hoisted out.

" 'In heaven's name, man,' cried Stubb, 'are you ramming home a cartridge there?—Avast, will ye!' 'Stand clear of the tackle,' cried a voice like the bursting of a rocket.

"Almost at the same instant, with a thunder boom, the enormous mass dropped into the sea, like Niagara's Table Rock into the whirlpool; the suddenly relieved hull rolled away from it, too far down her glittering copper; and all caught their breath, as half-swinging—now over the sailors' heads, and now over the water—Daggoo, through a thick mist of spray, was dimly beheld clinging to the pendulous tackles, while poor buried-alive Tashtego was sinking utterly down to the bottom of the sea.

"But hardly had the blinding vapor cleared away, when a naked figure with a boarding-sword in its hand, was for one swift moment seen hovering over the bulwarks. The next, a loud splash announced that my brave Queequeg had dived to the rescue.

"One packed rush was made to the side, and every eye counted every ripple, as moment followed moment, and no sign of either the sinker or the diver could be seen. Some hands now jumped into a boat alongside, and pushed a little off from the ship.

" 'Ha, ha,' cried Daggoo, all at once, from his now quiet swinging perch overhead; and looking farther off from the side, we saw an arm thrust upright from the blue waves; a sight strange to see, as an arm thrust forth from the grass over a grave.

" 'Both! both!—it is both!'—cried Daggoo again with a joyful shout; and soon after, Queequeg was seen boldly striking out with one hand, and with the other clutching the long hair of the Indian. Drawn into the waiting boat, they were quickly brought to the deck; but Tashtego was long in coming to, and Queequeg did not look very brisk.

"Now how had this noble rescue been accomplished? Why, diving after the slowly descending head, Queequeg, with his keen sword, had made side lunges near its bottom, so as to scuttle a large hole there; then dropping his sword, had thrust his long arm far inwards and upwards, and so hauled out our poor Tash by the head. He averred, that upon first thrusting in for him, a leg was presented; but well knowing that was not as it ought to be, and might occasion great trouble;—he had thrust back the leg, and by a dexterous heave and toss, had wrought a somerset upon the Indian; so that with the next trial, he came forth in the good old way—head foremost. As for the great head itself, that was doing as well as could be expected.

"And thus, through the courage and great skill in obstetrics of Queequeg, the deliverance, or rather delivery of Tashtego, was successfully accomplished, in the teeth too, of the most untoward and apparently hopeless impediments; which is a lesson by no means to be forgotten."

The lesson to be remembered, which is hidden in the above-given allegory, is, that the actors were *Sin,* personified by Tashtego; *Ignorance,* personified by Daggoo; and *Religion,* personified by Queequeg.

The responsibility for the predicament of the man of sin, is somewhat in doubt; the Palmist said; —*"Surely thou didst set them in slippery places; thou castedst them down into destruction."** But Ishmael was not sure whether it was because "the place where he stood was so treacherous and oozy; or whether the Evil One himself would have it to fall out so, without stating his particular reason."

Be that as it may, the man of *Sin* was sinking to perdition; his escape was impossible on account of *Ignorance;* but *Religion,* armed with the "sword of the spirit,"† rescued the perishing, by performing a Caesarean operation on the whale's head, and thereby, through his "great skill in obstetrics," effected a re-birth of the sinner; all of which teaches the lesson:— *"Except a man be born again, he cannot see the Kingdom of God."*‡

A good example of the surreptitious interpola-

* Psalms, 73, 18.
† Ephesians, 6, 17.
‡ John, 3, 3.

tion of a hidden meaning, in the midst of straight narrative, is found in the dialogue between Stubb and Flask, while they were bringing the right whale to the ship. Stubb had been imposing upon Flask's credulity, by telling him that Fedallah was the devil; and, in answer to a question by Flask, Stubb said:—

"I don't know, Flask, but the devil is a curious chap, and a wicked one, I tell ye. Why they say as how he went sauntering into the old flagship once, switching his tail about, devilish easy and gentlemanlike, and inquiring if the old governor was at home. Well, he was at home, and asked the devil what he wanted. The devil, switching his hoofs, up and says, 'I want John.' 'What for?' says the old governor. 'What business is that of yours?' says the devil, getting mad,—'I want to use him.' 'Take him,' says the governor,—and by the Lord, Flask, if the devil didn't give John the Asiatic Cholera before he got through with him, I'll eat this whale in one mouthful."

This parable is a palpable paraphrase of the prologue of the *Book of Job*. The "old flagship," symbolized the earth; the "old governor," represented the Lord, and John, of course, took the character of Job,—even the first two letters of their names are the same. The impudence of the devil, as described by Stubb, may be compared with the impudence of Satan, in the Biblical version;—

"And the Lord said unto Satan:—'Whence comest thou?' Then Satan answered the Lord and said;—'From going to and fro in the earth, and from walking up and down in it!'"* Moreover, the complaisance of the "old governor," in consenting to the devil's proposition to do whatever he pleased with John, follows the Scriptural text closely;— "And the Lord said unto Satan;—'Behold, all that he hath is in thy power.'† . . . So Satan went forth from the presence of the Lord, and smote Job with sore boils from the sole of his foot unto his crown."‡ The culmination of the afflictions heaped upon Job, by Satan, is paralleled by the Asiatic cholera, which the devil gave John.

A further observation, by Stubb, upon the same topic, contains another covert thrust at orthodoxy.

"Damn the devil, Flask; do you suppose that I'm afraid of the devil? Who's afraid of him except the old governor, who daren't catch him and put him in double darbies, as he deserves, but lets him go about kidnapping people. Aye, and signed a bond with him, that all the people the devil kidnapped, he'd roast for him. There's a governor." This is a variation on the old question;—"Why doesn't God kill the devil?" And the last sentence;—"There's a governor," with proper em-

* Job, 1, 7.
† Job, 1, 12.
‡ Job, 2, 7.

phasis, reveals Melville's opinion of the theological scheme.

Another parable may be found in the story of the whale's skeleton which was worshipped as a god, and which has been mentioned some pages back.

Ishmael, or Melville, cut a measuring rod, and proceeded to take the dimensions of the skeleton, but the priests discovered him in the act. " 'How now!' they shouted; 'Dar'st thou measure this our god! That's for us!' 'Aye priests—well, how long do you make him?' But hereupon a fierce contest rose among them, concerning feet and inches; they cracked each other's sconces with their yardsticks."

A casual reader may be amused by the extravagant fancy of Solomon Island priests belaboring each other with yardsticks; but such an absurdity is a sure sign that another meaning is hidden in the lines.

It should be noted that the priests claimed as their prerogative, the sole right to determine the attributes of their god,—with the implication that such arrogation is peculiar to ecclesiastics. Moreover, the contradictory opinions maintained by the priests were based upon their several conflicting measurements.

Now, as a "yardstick" is a familiar symbol for individual mental capacity; the scene presents, in parable, a satire on the ferocity of sectarian hatred, and it also teaches that each individual forms his own conception of God.

This general subjectivity of mankind, is noted by Stubb, when he commented upon the various interpretations of the symbols on the doubloon, for he said;—"There's another rendering now; but still one text. All sorts of men in one kind of world, you see." Captain Ahab also noted this same psychological trait, when he concluded;— "This round gold is but the image of the rounder globe, which, like a magician's glass, to each and every man in turn, but mirrors back his own mysterious self."*

The doctrines of Swedenborg, also received Melville's attention; an instance of which is here given;—

"Hither, and thither, on high, glided the snow-white wings of small unspeckled birds; these were the gentle thoughts of the feminine air; but to and fro in the deep, far down in the bottomless blue, rushed mighty leviathans, sword-fish and sharks; and these were the strong, troubled, murderous thinkings of the masculine sea."

The significance of the foregoing mystical flight, is apparent, when interpreted according to *The Language of Parable*,† which is an elucidation of

* Note 4.
† The Language of Parable, Rev. Wm. L. Worcester.

Swedenborg's *Doctrine of Correspondences.* From it we learn that;—"*Birds* correspond to the affections for thinking spiritually; for thinking of human life and the principles that relate to it." And also, "thought which looks at life from the spiritual side, is represented by *birds*, because they inhabit the *air*, which corresponds to *spiritual truth*."

As for the sea, we find that;—"*Water* corresponds to truth of *natural science; of* worldly industries. *Fishes are scientifics*, because their habits of life correspond to the gathering of material facts, which when classified, constitute *science.* Large fish eat the smaller ones, which corresponds to the *generalizing* mind making use of the material acquired by the less able minds. Hence, *large fish* are *generals or universals of scientifics. . . .* The water in which they live, is like an atmosphere of merely natural, worldly thought."

According to Swedenborg, the whale enjoys a very high correspondence; for it not only dominates the medium of natural, worldly thoughts; but can also enjoy the air and sunshine of spiritual thoughts.

Melville, apparently, conceived of a still rarer medium for human thought, when he said;—"Methinks that in looking at things spiritual, we are too much like oysters observing the sun through the water, and thinking that thick water the thinnest air."

Melville frequently made use of the analogy between a weaver, and the Creator, of which the most notable example may be found in a pleading for light upon the inscrutable mysteries,—the cause, and purpose, and end of all. This petition or prayer is of such rare beauty of imagery, and depth of feeling, that it should not be overlooked, for it is doubtful if this old and well-worn metaphor has ever been presented in a finer setting.

"It was a wondrous sight. The wood was green as mosses of the Icy Glen; the trees stood high and haughty, feeling their living sap; the industrious earth beneath was as a weaver's loom, with a gorgeous carpet on it, whereof the ground-vine tendrils formed the warp and woof, and the living flowers the figures. All the trees, with their laden branches; all the shrubs, and ferns, and grasses; the message-carrying air; all these unceasingly were active. Through the lacings of the leaves, the great sun seemed a flying shuttle weaving the unwearied verdure. Oh, busy weaver! unseen weaver!—pause!—one word!—whither flows the fabric? what palace may it deck? wherefore all these ceaseless toilings? Speak, weaver! stay thy hand! —but one single word with thee! Nay—the shuttle flies—the figures float from forth the loom; the freshet-rushing carpet for ever slides away. The weaver-god, he weaves; and by that weaving is he deafened, that he hears no mortal

voice; and by that humming, we too, who look
on the loom are deafened; and only when we escape it shall we hear the thousand voices that speak
through it."

X

MANY religions and philosophies are alluded to by Melville, with the implication that none of them held the answer to the eternal question.

The fire-worshipping religion of Zorpaster is the subject of some very exalted prose, in the chapter entitled; "Candles"; and the old gods of India are recognized in the chapter devoted to "The Dying Whale."

The doctrine of the transmigration of the soul is touched upon, several times. It is implied in the words of Pip, who asked Queequeg, who was thought to be dying;—"Poor rover! Will ye never have done with all this weary roving? Where go ye now?" The analogy between that doctrine, and the heart-breaking experience of cleaning the ship, only to have it messed up immediately, by another whale, is given in the lines;—

"Yet this is life. For hardly have we mortals by long toilings extracted from this world's vast bulk its small but valuable sperm; and then, with weary patience, cleansed ourselves from its defilements, and learned to live in clean tabernacles of the soul; hardly is this done, when—*There she blows!*— the ghost is spouted up, and away we sail to fight some other world, and go through young life's old routine again.

"O! the metempsychosis! O! Pythagoras! that in bright Greece, two thousand years ago, did die, so wise, so good, so mild; I sailed with thee along the Peruvian coast, last voyage,—and foolish as I am, I taught thee, a green simple boy, how to splice a rope."

The possibility of losing one's identity, through being absorbed into a universal life, was illustrated by the description of the danger at the masthead, as follows;—

"But while this sleep is on ye, move your foot an inch; slip your hold at all; and your identity comes back in horror. . . . And perhaps, at midday, in the fairest weather, with one half-throttled shriek, you drop through the transparent air into the summer sea, no more to rise forever. Heed it well ye Pantheists."

Melville also shunned the prospect of annihilation, for, in speaking of the mystic qualities of the color, white, he asks;—

"Is it by its indefiniteness it shadows forth the heartless voids and immensities of the universe, and thus stabs us in the back with the thought of annihilation, when beholding the white depths of the milky way?"

Plato was dismissed with the question:—"How many, think ye, have fallen into Plato's honey head, and sweetly perished there?" Plato's exoneration of God from all responsibility for sin and suffering, did not harmonize with Melville's pessimistic convictions.

The Stoic philosophy was equally unacceptable to Melville, and his opinion of the Stoics is disclosed in the title of a chapter devoted to that school. The chapter is entitled; "The Hyena," and it begins;—

"There are certain queer times and occasions in this strange mixed affair we call life, when a man takes this whole universe for a vast practical joke. . . . Nothing dispirits, and nothing seems worth while disputing . . . and as for small difficulties and worryings, prospects of sudden disaster, peril of life and limb; all these, and death itself, seem to him only sly, good-natured hits and jolly punches in the side, bestowed by the unseen and unaccountable old joker."

Now, as a joke is usually followed by a laugh, and as some hyenas are said to laugh, Melville, with a little false logic, implies that a man who can laugh at misfortune, is *a Hyena;*—he could not comprehend that such a man is beyond the reach of Fate.

The foregoing description of the Stoics, further confirms the identification of Flask, as their representative; for the analysis of his character, in the chapter, "Knights and Squires," includes these lines;—

"This ignorant unconscious fearlessness of his,

made him a little waggish in the matter of whales;
he followed these fish for the fun of it; and a
three years' voyage round Cape Horn, was only a
jolly joke that lasted that length of time."

It was consistent with Melville's sensitive and
sympathetic nature, to dislike a philosophy that
taught indifference to human suffering; but, nevertheless, it was his greatest misfortune to lack the
requisite drop of Stoic blood, and the saving sense
of humor that makes life worth living. In fact, he
said;—"That mortal man who hath more of joy
than sorrow in him, that mortal man cannot be true
—not true, or undeveloped." Furthermore, the
serious bent of his nature is revealed in the following lines, which ostensibly describe the Quaker
idiom, or at least, its origin, but which in reality,
describe himself.

"And when these things unite in a man of greatly
superior force, with a globular brain and a ponder-
ous heart; who has also by the stillness and seclu-
sion of many long night-watches in the remotest
waters, and beneath constellations never seen here
in the north, been led to think untraditionally and
independently; receiving all nature's sweet or savage impressions fresh from her own virgin, volun-
tary and confiding breast, and thereby chiefly, but
with some help from accidental advantages, to
learn a bold and nervous lofty language—that man
makes one in a whole nation's census—a mighty

pageant creature, formed for noble tragedies. Nor will it at all detract from him, dramatically regarded, if either by birth or other circumstances, he have what seems a half wilful, over-ruling morbidness at the bottom of his nature. For all men tragically great are made so through a certain morbidness."

Melville was also of the opinion that;—"The truest of all books is Solomon's, and Ecclesiastes is the fine hammered steel of woe." But Melville lived his life before he could learn the true meaning of Ecclesiastes, as revealed by the late Morris Jastrow, Jr. That authority proves that the book was not written by Solomon, but by a sceptic, under the pseudonym of "Kaholeth." And Dr. Jastrow also shows that the original text was literally swamped, by the Rabbis, with contradictory and neutralizing phrases, for the object of counteracting the materialistic and anti-religious spirit of the book, and the cynical lesson which it taught, which is;—"Life has no goal,—therefore smile at life and pity those who live under the delusion that life is a very serious business."*

Melville's philosophy was chiefly a philosophy of gloom, and his consolation, apparently, was in his belief that morbidness and genius are inseparable. Yet, at times, he must have been conscious of a temperamental deficiency, for, the following

* A Gentle Cynic, Morris Jastrow, Jr.

[117]

paragraph, is, in a measure, a contradiction of what has already been stated.

"However, a good laugh is a mighty good thing; and rather too scarce a good thing; more's the pity. So, if any one man, in his own proper person, affords stuff for a good joke, to anybody, let him not be backward, but let him cheerfully allow himself to spend and be spent in that way. And the man that has anything bountifully laughable about him, be sure there is more in that man than you perhaps think for."

Although an extreme introvert, Melville also doubted that his mind was an all-sufficient kingdom, for he admitted;—

"I have perceived that in all cases man must eventually lower, or at least shift, his conceit of attainable felicity; not placing it anywhere in the intellect or the fancy; but in the wife, the heart, the bed, the table, the saddle, the fireside, the country." But he could not adapt himself, for he put the words in Captain Ahab's mouth, who personified the *Intellect*, and said:—"I can ne'er enjoy. Gifted with high perception, I lack the low, enjoying power; damned, most subtly and most malignantly damned in the midst of Paradise."

However, Melville did his thinking for himself, and he scorned a beaten track, as shown when he exultingly pointed out;—"There's your utility of traditions; there's the story of your obstinate survival of old beliefs, never bottomed on the earth, and not now even hovering in the air." He also repelled proselyting in the name of authority, for to him; "thrusted light is worse than presented pistols." He gloried in his independence of thought, and was thoroughly self-reliant, as his words clearly show;—"I rejoice in my spine, as in the firm audacious staff of that flag which I fling half out to the world," and "None but cowards send down their brain-trucks in tempest time."

Apparently no creed or system could satisfy Melville, so he advised rejecting them all, as illustrated by the analogy of the whales' heads careening the ship;—"So, when on one side you hoist in Locke's head, you go over that way, but now on the other side, you hoist in Kant's, and you come back again; but in very poor plight. Thus some minds for ever keep trimming boat. O, ye foolish, throw all these thunderheads overboard, and then you will float light and free." Moreover, he surmised;—"Perhaps to be true philosophers, we mortals should not be conscious of so living, or so striving";—in other words, he suspected that philosophers are born,—not made.

Science, with its materialistic tendencies, held no appeal for Melville. He disposed of that branch of learning, with the remark;—"Physiognomy, like every other human science, is but a passing fable."

Melville was intellectually honest, as is shown by Captain Ahab, who personified the *Intellect*, and who did not know what faith is. "Faith, Sir, I've—" said the carpenter. "Faith? What's that?" inquired Ahab.

Since faith and reason are incompatible, Melville preferred to rely upon reason, as far as he could go, and beyond the reach of reason, he hoped for intuition.

An appraisal of an author's beliefs and disbeliefs, based upon his works of fiction, is somewhat hazardous, as Alfred Noyes points out;—"When have critics known the Poet from his creatures . . .? How many cite Polonius to their sons and call it Shakespeare?"* Therefore all conclusions, in that respect, are subject to the hypothetical "If." That is, *if* Melville, under cover of his characters, confessed his personal convictions, we find that he believed in natural religion, which is merely the bond or obligation and sense of duty which we feel from the relation in which we stand to some superior power.

He also believed in a malignant Fate, and in the symbolical correspondence between material and spiritual things. But he did not believe in any theological scheme invented by man; for doctrinal religion is the object of his allegorical satire.

As to a hereafter, he was in doubt, if the words

* Tales of the Mermaid Tavern.

in Father Mapple's sermon reveal his attitude:— "Mortal or immortal, here I die. . . . I leave eternity to Thee; for what is man that he should live out the lifetime of his God?" And furthermore, when Queequeg's coffin was made into a lifebuoy, Captain Ahab soliloquized;—"A lifebuoy of a coffin! Does it go further? Can it be that in some spiritual sense the coffin is, after all, but an immortality-preserver! I'll think of that. But no. So far gone am I in the dark side of earth, that its other side, the theoretical bright one, seems but uncertain twilight to me."

Melville not only found that "the dead, blind wall butts all inquiring heads at last"; but his metaphysical travels brought him, by a different route, to the same *Port of Agnosticism*, that is reached by the conscientious scientist, as his non-committal words attest:—

"Through all the thick mists of the dim doubts in my mind, divine intuitions now and then shoot, enkindling my fog with a heavenly ray. And for this I thank God; for all have doubts; many deny; but doubts or denials, few along with them have intuitions. Doubts of all things earthly, and intuitions of some things heavenly; this combination makes neither believer nor infidel, but makes a man who regards them both with equal eye."

XI

THE leading parable, or allegorical crusade, represented by a hunt for a white whale, describes an attempt to ameliorate human conditions, in accordance with the belief, held by many religions, that a savior will appear at some time or other, to relieve the world of its troubles.

It is apparent from the many analogies in the text, that Captain Ahab, in his hidden character, championed the cause of mankind. He is associated with Anacharsis Clootz, in these words:— "An Anacharsis deputation . . . accompanying old Ahab in the *Pequod*, to lay the world's grievances before that bar, from which not very many of them ever come back." The bar of *Unreason* is implied here. This Anacharsis Clootz, with the hope of redressing the wrongs of humanity, headed a delegation, from all nations, to the Bar of the Assembly, in Paris, styling himself;—"The Orator of the Human Race."

Perseus, according to Melville, rescued Andromeda from a *whale*, and the analogy between Ahab and that classic champion, lies in the line:—"his whole high, broad form seemed made of solid bronze, and shaped like Cellini's cast Perseus."

And during the storm, Captain Ahab had in mind, Prometheus, stealing fire from heaven.

Prometheus, too, was a defender of the human race; he taught mankind the arts of life—as when Ahab magnetized the sail-maker's needle. Prometheus defied the gods,—so did Captain Ahab, crying out;—"Ye great gods . . . I laugh and hoot at ye." The identification is quite clear in another passage;—"God help thee, old man, thy thoughts have created a creature in thee; and he whose intense thinking thus makes him a Prometheus; a vulture feeds upon his heart forever." In short, Captain Ahab's character, in its relation to the supernatural expedition, is a composite of all the historical and mythical rebels against Destiny.

In every myth which tells of a conflict between a defender of mankind, and a predatory monster, Melville, by curious argument, maintains that the monster was a whale. This is done, ostensibly, to prove the eligibility of such heroes as Perseus, St. George, Hercules, and others, to membership in the "Whaleman's Club," but the ulterior purpose is to show that the principal, inimical to humanity, meaning *Fate*, is invariably symbolized by a *whale*.

The argument for this expedition, as gathered from the text, is that mankind is the helpless victim of predestinated suffering, and for all that misery in the world, some unspeakable power is responsible. This power, otherwise *Fate*, is represented by the White Whale, which is, therefore, Fate's symbol, or agent, for;—"All things that most ex-

[123]

asperate and outrage mortal man, all these things are bodiless, but only bodiless as objects, not as agents. There's a most special, a most cunning, Oh, a most malicious difference."

Captain Ahab, in his hidden character of a practical redeemer, feels in his own heart the total sum of human suffering, and seeks out the living symbol of all that suffering, and endeavors to destroy it, intending thereby, to relieve the human race of its hereditary curse; for;—"Ahab was intent upon an audacious, immitigable and supernatural revenge." "He piled upon the whale's white hump, the sum of all the general rage and hate felt by his whole race from Adam down." "All the subtile demonisms of life and thought; all evil, to crazy Ahab, were visibly personified and made practically assailable in Moby Dick."

Captain Ahab explained his working theory to his mates, as follows;—

"All visible objects are but pasteboard masks, but in each event—in the living act, the undoubted deed—there, some unknown, but still reasoning thing, puts forth the mouldings of its features from behind the unreasoning mask. If man will strike, strike through the mask. . . . That inscrutable thing is chiefly what I hate; and be the White Whale agent, or be the White Whale principal, I will wreak that hate upon him."* Briefly, the plan

* Note 5.

was *to annihilate Fate, by destroying the symbol of Fate.* It should also be noted, that the day on which this practical redeemer set out upon his mission to save the world, was Christmas Day, which is further corroboration of the implied fact that Captain Ahab assumed the character of a savior.

All throughout the voyage, the works of Fate are made manifest by what befalls the inhabitants of the other ships—which are also symbols of the world—that the *Pequod* meets.

The *Town-Ho's* story tells of the swift retribution which overtook a cruel mate,—signifying *the vengeance of Fate.*

Those on board the *Virgin*, without a drop of oil, felt *the parsimony of Fate.*

The captain of the *Rosebud*, who was a French perfumer, was persuaded to give away a bad-smelling whale, which, unknown to him, contained ambergris; and thus he was made a victim of the *irony of Fate.*

To those on board the *Samuel Enderby*, Fate brought *contentment.*

Fate gave *riches* to the crew of the *Bachelor*, with every container overflowing with oil.

To the father who was captain of the *Rachael*, and who lost his two young sons, Fate brought *sorrow.*

The ship, *Delight*, with her boats stove, and five

men lost, suffered the *malignity* of Fate. And all this good and evil was wrought by the *Whale*.

As the day of doom drew near, the text becomes more and more portentous and symbolical, for, "now almost the least heedful eye seemed to see some sort of cunning meaning in almost every sight." "The first man of the *Pequod* that mounted the mast to look out for the White Whale, on the White Whale's own peculiar ground; that man was swallowed up in the deep."

Ahab's hat was snatched from his head, by a sea hawk, which symbolized the uncrowning of a king, and another hawk flew away with the flag at the main truck,—prophetic of defeat.

Heavenly guidance was rejected by the destruction of the quadrant;—" 'Curse thee, thou vain toy; and cursed be all things that cast man's eyes aloft. . . . Curse thee, thou quadrant,' dashing it to the deck, 'No longer will I guide my earthly way by thee.' "

Ahab then resorted to the earthly device of dead-reckoning, the weakness of which was shown by the breaking of the rotten log-line. "Has he not," said Starbuck, "dashed his heavenly quadrant,? and in these same perilous seas, gropes he not his way by mere dead-reckoning of the error-abounding log?"

The appearance of St. Elmo's fire, was another warning. Stubb cried;—"The corposants have mercy on us all," and Melville adds "In all my voyaging seldom have I heard a common oath when God's burning finger has been laid on the ship; when his 'Mene, Mene, Tekel Upharsin,' has been woven into the shrouds and the cordage."

On the occasion when; "a great rolling sea . . . stove in the boat's bottom, at the stern," Starbuck said to Stubb;—"Now mark his boat there, where is that stove. In the stern sheets, man; where he is wont to stand—his standpoint is stove, man."

"Believe ye men, in things called omens?" asked Ahab, "Then laugh aloud, and cry encore."

When Ahab made his final thrust at the White Whale, he reached the utmost height of defiance, for his last words were:—"Towards thee I roll, Thou all destroying but unconquering whale; to the last I grapple with thee; from hell's heart I stab at thee; for hate's sake I spit my last breath at thee."

In the allegorical catastrophe, in which *Fate destroyed the world*, it is significant that the personifications of *Ignorance, Religion,* and *Sin,* were the last to disappear.

The symbolism of the sky-hawk, which was dragged down by Tashtego, who personified *Sin*, is explained by Melville, in the words;—"the bird of heaven, with unearthly shrieks, and his imperial beak thrust upwards, and his whole captive form folded in the flag of Ahab, went down with the ship, which, like Satan, would not sink to hell, till she had dragged a living part of heaven along with her."

In order to maintain the plausibility of the superficial narrative, Melville, in an epilogue, describes the escape of Ishmael, on the coffin-lifebuoy. This, for the sake of unity, is a well-advised separation from the allegorical catastrophe, from which no man escaped, for, "the great shroud of the sea rolled on as it rolled five thousand years ago."

There is an incident which should be noted for its intimate resemblance to Swedenborg's description of the manner in which Celestial intelligence is revealed to the inhabitants of the spiritual world. Spoken language is not used; instead; images of things in the natural world are shown as symbols, and the corresponding meanings are comprehended infallibly. Likewise, during the encounter with the White Whale, on the second day, Fedallah, who personified the *Future*, disappeared; but on the third day, when the whale was again attacked, the body of the Parsee was discovered entangled among the numerous lines which were wrapped around the whale. Thus is the *Future bound up with Fate*.

When the hidden image in a puzzle picture is finally discovered, it immediately becomes obtrusively obvious. In much the same way, the significance of *"The Town Ho's Story"* appears in the light of its surrounding chapters, for that story contains the Fate theme, which later, is elaborated and developed in the major story.

This story tells of a sailor who was killed by Moby Dick, and the hand of Fate in that calamity, is insisted upon, again, and again. Moreover, the symbol of Fate is all but plainly stated, for, in answer to the question; "Whom call you Moby Dick?" the reply is;—"A very white, and famous, and most deadly immortal monster."

The victim is mentioned as "the predestinated mate," and it is also said of him, that; "the fool had been branded for the slaughter by the gods." Compare the last quotation with the following:— "When branded Ahab gives chase to Moby Dick."

The similarity of the two plots is further confirmed by the statement that; "A strange fatality pervades the whole career of these events, as if verily mapped out before the world itself was charted," and its repetition, when Captain Ahab said:—"This whole act's immutably decreed. 'Twas rehearsed by thee and me a billion years before this ocean rolled."

XII

THERE is another parable in *Moby Dick*, second only, in interest to the attempt to annihilate Fate, for it proves the infallibility of Fate. It is, in fact, complementary to the main parable, like an accompaniment to a musical theme.

This parable is founded upon the history of Ahab, King of Israel, which composes the most fatalistic story in the Bible. It tells of how that King, who, after stealing Naboth's vineyard, was told by Elijah, the prophet, that;—"In the place where the dogs licked the blood of Naboth, shall dogs lick thy blood."*

Some time afterwards, King Ahab, with the aid of Jehoshaphat, King of Judea, planned a campaign against the Syrians, at Ramoth-gilead. The two kings, wishing to ascertain if their prospects for success were favorable, summoned King Ahab's prophets for consultation. These prophets all promised success, for they knew that King Ahab would punish them if they foretold anything unfavorable to the enterprise. But Jehoshaphat was not entirely satisfied, so he asked for another prophet. King Ahab then sent for Micaiah, of whom he said;—"I hate him; for he doth not prophecy good concerning me, but evil."†

* 1 Kings, 21, 19.
† 1 Kings, 22, 8.

After the subsidized prophets had given their favorable forecast, Micaiah, in proof of his contention that the optimists were false, discredited their words by relating what he saw in a celestial vision.

"I saw the Lord sitting on His throne, and all the host of heaven standing by Him on His right hand and on His left. And the Lord said; Who shall persuade Ahab, that he may go up and fall at Ramoth-gilead? And one said on this manner, and another said on that manner. And there came forth a spirit, and stood before the Lord, and said; I will persuade him. And the Lord said unto him, Wherewith? And he said; I will go forth and I will be a lying spirit in the mouth of all his prophets. And He said; Thou shalt persuade him, and prevail also, go forth and do so."*

Thus was Ahab, King of Israel, marked by Fate; for the lying spirit did prevail; and the two kings prepared for battle. But King Ahab thought to mislead Fate, and to disprove the adverse prophecy; so he disguised himself, and, to make the deception complete, Jehoshaphat attired himself in King Ahab's robes.

However, the subterfuge was of no avail; for, "a certain man drew a bow at a venture, and smote the King of Israel between the joints of the harness."† And so Fate unerringly found him out, with what was seemingly, a mere random shot.

* 1 Kings, 22, 19-22.
† 1 Kings, 22, 34.

The first intimation of an analogy between Captain Ahab, and Ahab, King of Israel, and the prophecies concerning them, occurs in the dialogue between Captain Peleg and Ishmael.

" 'Ahab of old,' said Peleg, 'Thou knowest was a crowned King.' " Ishmael replied; "And a very wicked one. When that wicked king was slain, the dogs, did they not lick his blood?"

" 'Come hither to me—hither, hither,' said Peleg, with a significance in his eye that almost startled me. 'Look ye, lad; never say that on board the *Pequod*. Never say it anywhere. Captain Ahab did not name himself. 'Twas a foolish, ignorant whim of his crazy widowed mother, who died when he was only a twelvemonth old. And yet the old squaw Tisig, at Gay Head, said that the name would somehow prove prophetic.' "

Another, and a more direct association of the two Ahabs, may be seen, when, "Little Flask enters King Ahab's presence, in the character of Abjectus, the slave," for "how could one look at Ahab then seated on that tripod of bones, without bethinking him of the royalty it symbolized?"

The way in which Ahab, King of Israel was marked by Fate, has been told; the mark of Fate that Captain Ahab carried, is described as follows;—

"Threading its way down from among his grey hairs, and continuing right down one side of his tawny scorched face and neck, till it disappeared in his clothing, you saw a slender rod-like mark, lividly whitish."

This mark was placed upon Ahab, according to a superstitious old sailor; "during an elemental strife at sea." But the old Manxman, who personified *Prescience*, stated;

"That if ever Captain Ahab should be tranquilly laid out,—which might hardly come to pass —. . . then, whoever should do that last office for the dead, would find a birthmark on him from crown to sole."

There were two true prophets in the affair of Ahab, King of Israel, namely, Elijah, and Micaiah; and likewise there were two true prophets for Captain Ahab. The first one was also named Elijah, and he is described in a chapter, entitled; "The Prophet." He is referred to, by Ishmael, as a "crazy man," and also as "the prophet of the wharves." This true prophet said to Ishmael; "with his ambiguous, half-hinting, half-revealing, shrouded sort of talk;" " 'Oh, I was going to warn ye against—but never mind. Good-bye to ye. Shan't see ye again very soon, I guess; unless it's before the Grand Jury' ";—by which he meant the Day of Judgement,—having foreseen the catastrophe.

The other true prophet, was the lunatic, Gabriel, on board the ship *Jeroboam*, who, referring to a mate of that vessel, who had recently been killed by Moby Dick, cried to Captain Ahab;—" 'Thou art soon going that way. . . . Think of thy whale boat stoven and sunk! Beware of the horrible tail, . . . Think, think of the blasphemer—dead, and down there!—beware of the blasphemer's end!' " "His credulous disciples believed that he had specifically fore-announced it." (The death of the mate.) But Captain Ahab cursed him, just as King Ahab had cursed his own true prophets.

Melville holds consistently to his theory of intuition, for Elijah, Gabriel, and Pip, were, all of them, crazy. However, the madness in the book; especially that of old Ahab, is but an artful device for supporting or covering up the bizarre fantasy that is woven into the ostensible story.* Moreover, Melville stated, at the outset, that *reason* would be but a sleeping-partner-shipmate, so far as this narrative is concerned.

In taking up Fedallah, the Parsee, again, it may be said, that this character, as well as that of Captain Ahab, is composite; for in addition to personifying the *Future*, Fedallah was Captain Ahab's *Genius*. He was also a composite genius, for he not only guided Ahab through life, and conducted him out of the world, and into the next, at the close of his career, according to the Roman belief; but he partook of the nature of the genii of the East, as

* Note 6.

shown by his intimate association with fire,—as a fire-worshipping Parsee. Also, in the role of *False prophet*, he became Ahab's *Evil genius*.

Melville gave considerable space to the identification of Fedallah as Ahab's genius, from which a few excerpts are here given.

"Whence he came into a mannerly world like this; by what sort of unaccountable tie he soon evinced himself to be linked with Ahab's peculiar fortunes; nay, so far as to have some sort of a half-hinted influence; Heaven knows; but it might have been even authority over him; all this none knew." "Such an added gliding strangeness began to invest the thin Fedallah now; such ceaseless shudderings shook him; that the men looked dubious at him; half uncertain, as it seemed, whether indeed he were a mortal substance, or else a tremulous shadow cast upon the deck by some unseen being's body." ". . . a potent spell seemed secretly to join the twain. . . ." "Ahab in his scuttle, the Parsee by the mainmast; but still fixedly gazing upon each other; as in the Parsee, Ahab saw his forethrown shadow, in Ahab, the Parsee, his abandoned substance." "Still again both seemed yoked together. . . ." A merging of the two identities is suggested in the line;—"Ahab chanced so to stand, that the Parsee occupied his shadow; while if the Parsee's shadow was there at all, it seemed only to blend with, and lengthen Ahab's." Fedallah was also spoken of to Ahab, as; "thy evil shadow."

Captain Ahab's impending doom was revealed to him in a symbolical dream; but Fedallah, in the role of a false prophet, with a lying spirit in his mouth, assured Ahab of success in his enterprise, by unwittingly giving him a misleading interpretation of the dream.

"Started from his slumber, Ahab, face to face, saw the Parsee; and hooped round by the gloom of night they seemed the last men in a flooded world. 'I have dreamed it again,' said he.

'Of the hearses?   Have I not said, old man, that neither hearse nor coffin can be thine?'

'And who are hearsed that die on the sea?'

'But I said, old man, that ere thou couldst die on this voyage, two hearses must verily be seen by thee on the sea; the first not made by mortal hands; and the visible wood of the last one must be grown in America.'

'Aye, aye, a strange sight that, Parsee;—a hearse and its plumes floating over the ocean with waves for pallbearers.   Ha, such a sight we shall not soon see.'

'Believe it or not, thou canst not die till it be seen, old man.'

'And what was that saying about thyself?'

'Though it comes to the last, I shall still go before thee, thy pilot.'

'And when thou art so gone before—if that ever befall—then ere I can follow, thou must still appear to me, to pilot me still? Was it not so? Well, then, did I believe all ye say, Oh my pilot, I have here two pledges that I shall yet slay Moby Dick and survive it.'

'Take another pledge, old man,' said the Parsee, as his eyes lighted up like fire-flies in the gloom— 'Hemp only can kill thee.'

'The gallows ye mean.—I am immortal then, on land and on sea.' " And so did the lying spirit in the mouth of Fedallah, Ahab's false prophet prevail, and persuade him to persist in his audacious undertaking. It should also be remembered, that it is the duty of one's genius to pilot him out of this world and into the next.

There is another analogy between the two Ahabs;—the analogy of special weapons for their particular purposes.

Zedekiah, one of King Ahab's false prophets;— "made him horns of iron; and he said;—Thus saith the Lord, with these shalt thou push the Syrians until thou have consumed them."*

Captain Ahab's special weapon, was a harpoon, made for him by the blacksmith. It was made of material furnished by the captain, who;

". . . flinging a pouch upon the anvil, said;— 'Look ye blacksmith, these are the gathered nail-

* 1 Kings, 22, 11.

[137]

stubbs of the steel shoes of racing horses.' 'Horse-shoe stubbs, sir? Why Captain Ahab, thou hast here then, the best and stubbornest stuff we blacksmith ever work.'" "Racing horses" are silent symbols of the abstract quality, *Speed*, which is very desirable to have in a harpoon; but all that the blacksmith could see, was the material quality;—the toughness of the metal.

The events of the prophecy, concerning Captain Ahab, were fulfilled, as specified; but according to their true meanings. Fedallah was the first to go. The next day, his corpse, tied to the whale, was seen by Ahab, and so he saw the hearse not made by mortal hands. And when he saw the ship sinking, filled with men, he saw the second hearse, made of wood grown in America.

Another analogous detail may be seen in the presence of the sharks, snapping at the oars of Ahab's boat. These sharks represent the dogs that licked King Ahab's blood, at the Pool of Samaria.

This analogy is remarked several times;—once when Stubb said;—"I saw some sharks astern,—St. Bernard dogs, you know." And Melville asserts that during a sea-fight;—"Sharks will be seen longingly gazing up to the ship's decks, like hungry dogs round a table." The analogy is confirmed further, by Melville's answer to his own question;—"Does the ocean furnish any fish that in disposition answers to the sagacious kindness of the dog? The accursed shark alone, can in any generic respect be said to bear comparative analogy to him."

The part which the sharks were intended to play, may be surmised from Ahab's query;—" 'But who can tell'—he muttered,—'Whether these sharks swim to feast on the whale, or on Ahab?' " And it should be noted also, that the sharks "seemed to follow that one boat without molesting the others."

The finishing stroke, involving "hemp," was a mere casual circumstance, as commonplace as the random arrow that killed Ahab, King of Israel. It was seemingly, an accidental loop in the whale line attached to Moby Dick. "Ahab stopped to clear it; he did clear it; but the flying turn caught him round the neck, and voicelessly as Turkish mutes bow-string their victims, he was shot out of the boat, ere the crew knew he was gone." And so both Ahabs tried to circumvent Fate; but both were destroyed.

Josephus, it was who wrote, commenting on the death of Ahab, King of Israel;—"We may also, from what happened to this king, consider the power of Fate; that there is no way of avoiding it, even when we know it. It creeps upon human souls, and flatters them with pleasing hopes, till it leads them about to a place whence it will be too hard for them. Accordingly Ahab appears to have been deceived thereby, till he disbelieved those that predicted his defeat; but by giving credit to such as foretold what was grateful to him, he was slain."

END

NOTES

1. Another mystic, Lafcadio Hearn, held a similar belief; "All that we have taken for substance, is only shadow; the physical is the unreal; and the outer man is the ghost."

Lafcadio Hearn, by Nina Kennard

2. The differentiation of the Man-God from the God-Man was noted also by the Russian ex-monk Bazakuloff, founder of the sect of "Little White Cows," as may be seen in the following excerpt from *South Wind*, by Norman Douglass: "About this time, too, he (Bazakuloff) would sometimes prophesy, and undergo long periods of motionless self-abstraction. At the end of one of these latter, after tasting no food or drink for three and a half hours, he gave utterance to what was afterwards known as the First Revelation. It ran to this effect:—'The Man-God is the Man-God, and not the God-Man.' Asked how he arrived at so stupendous an aphorism, he answered that it just came to him."

3. Lafcadio Hearn felt the same way about the sea:—"I must confess, that when I am either in the sea or upon it, I cannot fully persuade myself that it is not alive—a conscious and a hostile power. Reason for the time being, avails nothing against this fancy."

Ghostly Japan

4. A similar idea occurred to Lafcadio Hearn:—"Each of us is truly a mirror, imaging something of the universe,—reflecting also the reflection of ourselves in that universe."

Out of the East

5. Somewhere, Goethe held a like theory:—"The intellectual, not satisfied with what is put before him, considers as a mask, everything that presents itself to his senses. He knows that a higher spiritual life, roguishly obstinate, hides itself behind the visible cloak."

[141]

6. Captain Ahab was cloaked with madness for the same reason that Don Quixote was endowed with lunacy, for, according to Henry Hallam, in his *Literature of Europe;*—"It was a necessary consequence that the hero (Don Quixote) must be represented as literally insane, since his conduct would have been extravagant beyond the probability of fiction, on any other hypothesis."

7. John Tyndall gives the same advice in somewhat similar metaphor. "It is perfectly possible for you and me to purchase intellectual peace at the price of intellectual death. The world is not without refuges of this description; nor it is wanting in persons who seek their shelter, and try to persuade others to do the same. The unstable and the weak have yielded and will yield to this persuasion, and they to whom repose is sweeter than truth. But I would exhort you to refuse the offered shelter, and to scorn the base repose—to accept, if the choice be forced upon you, commotion before stagnation, the breezy leap of the torrent before the foetid stillness of the swamp."

Fragments of Science

8. Don Quixote also found consolation in a similar line of reasoning:—"I would have thee know, Sancho, that wounds given with instruments that are accidentally in the hand are no affront: thus it is expressly written in the law of combat that, if a shoemaker strike a person with the last he has in his hand, though it be really of wood, it will not therefore be said that the person thus beaten with it was cudgelled."

ANALYSIS OF THE ALLEGORICAL PLAY

THE list of emotions, as set down opposite to the actors in the allegorical play, may appear to be arbitrarily determined; but the interpretation will be found to be justified, if the meanings of the lines are analyzed.

Words and actions are the sensible manifestations of thoughts and emotions, therefore, the kind of emotion which inspired the words in the play, may be discovered by the nature of the words themselves. Moreover, an interesting contrast of emotions may be noted, for many are followed by their antonyms, and it is also interesting, that many of the emotions are appropriate to the racial characteristics of the speakers.

The play begins with a song pertaining to love, and, as *love* is a universal emotion, all the players sing the chorus.

In contrast with the sentimentalism of the opening lines, the 1st Nantucket sailor, who objected to them, sings a song of a practical character, descriptive of the work expected of whalemen, which is indicative of *duty*.

The imperious interruption of the song, by the Mate, on the quarter-deck, implies *authority*, and the immediate response by the 2nd Nantucket sailor, who called the watch below, shows *obedience*.

However, the sleeping sailors did not hear the summons of the 2nd Nantucket sailor, so the Dutch sailor advised him to make use of a copper pump, which would serve as a speaking trumpet, and which would amplify the sound of his voice; and he also advised him to go "At 'em again." This exemplifies *thoroughness*.

At this point, the French sailor, with characteristic gaiety, proposed "a jig or two," which shows that he possessed *initiative*.

But he was opposed by sleepy Pip, who was not interested, and who plainly showed his *indifference*.

Thereupon, the French sailor exhorted his shipmates to dance and "gallop into the double shuffle," with the assertion that "Merry's the word,"—a clear lead to the emotion, merriment, or *joy*.

In contrast, the Iceland sailor, who objected to the dancing floor, expressed *sorrow*, by saying;—"I'm sorry to throw cold water on the subject; but excuse me."

Also, the Maltese sailor asked to be excused, because there were no girls with whom to dance, and he questioned the power of *imagination*, by inquiring; "Who but a fool would take his left hand by his right, and say to himself, how d'ye do?"

The light-hearted Sicilian sailor, at the thought

of "girls and a green," would have been willing to "turn grasshopper," which is indicative of *frivolity*.

The Long Island sailor reproved his critical shipmates, with the admonition;—"Hoe corn when you may—All legs go to harvest soon," which suggests *opportunism*.

The Azore sailor, thereupon, started the dance with such impetuous animation, that he clearly expressed *enthusiasm*.

Pip, who was wide awake, by this time, pounded his tambourine so violently that the "jigglers" dropped off, which was a demonstration of *destructiveness*.

The China sailor, who then advised Pip to rattle his teeth and make a pagoda of himself, indulged in an Oriental *fantasy*.

The French sailor, who had become "merry mad," and proposed to jump through the hoop of Pip's tambourine, cried to his comrades;—"Split jibs! tear yourselves"; thereby personifying *ecstasy*.

The stoical Indian, Tashtego, refused to take part in the general gaiety, and plainly expressed his *apathy*.

The gloomy old Manx sailor was impressed by the thought that beneath the dancing men, were the bones of dead sailors;—a morbid expression of *grief*.

The dancing became so violent and exhausting, that the 3rd Nantucket sailor complained;—"This is worse than pulling after whales in a calm"; which shows that the merriment had been carried to *excess*.

The Lascar sailor was the first to notice the approach of a storm, and he commented upon its possible effect; which indicates *foresight*.

As the storm grew in intensity, and the white caps began to dance, the Maltese sailor compared them with women. "Now would all the waves were women, then I'd go drown, and chassee with them evermore! There's naught so sweet on earth —heaven may not match it";—thereby confessing to *passion*.

But the Sicilian sailor, after teasingly stirring the other's imagination to a higher pitch, added a short homily on *continence*, by saying;—"Not taste, observe ye, else comes satiety."

Without any apparent reason, the Tahitian sailor displayed his *patriotism*, in an apostrophe to Tahiti.

The Portuguese sailor marked the increasing intensity of the storm, in detail; which showed *observation*.

The Danish sailor did not fear the storm, because he had *confidence* in the mate at the wheel. "The mate there holds ye to it stiffly. He's no more afraid than the isle fort at Cattegat."

The 4th Nantucket sailor explained the necessity for *boldness*, by quoting Captain Ahab, to the effect, that to "Kill a squall—fire your ship right into it."

The English sailor, in admiration of Captain Ahab's "grand" qualities, announced;—"We are the lads to hunt him up his whale"; which was an expression of *loyalty*.

All the sailors cried "Aye! Aye!" to that assertion, thereby assuming that they were all equal to the task, which shows their *self-esteem*.

The old Manx sailor gave a hint of possible disaster, by alluding to the captain's birthmark, and its likeness to a streak of lightning in the sky. He also remarked; "This is the sort of weather when brave hearts snap ashore, and keeled hulls split at sea," all of which constitutes *foreboding*.

Daggoo, then said;—"Who's afraid of black's afraid of me"; which implies that a dread of the dark, gives rise to *superstition*.

The Spanish sailor, taking advantage of the opportunity to insult Daggoo, sneered at the darkness of his race, thereby showing his *spitefulness*.

But Daggoo did not take offense, which was an exhibition of *forbearance*.

The St. Jago's sailor mused upon the aggressive attitude of the Spaniard; thereby indulging in *speculation*.

The 5th Nantucket sailor merely asked a question concerning the lightning, thereby evincing his *inquisitiveness*.

The Spanish sailor again insulted Daggoo, by comparing Daggoo's white teeth to the lightning; —a clear example of *malice*.

Daggoo, however, resented this attack, which showed his *anger*.

The Spanish sailor met him with the remark; "Knife thee heartily," in proof of his *quarrelsomeness*.

All the sailors cried;—"A row! a row! a row!" which goes to show that *excitement* is a common emotion.

Tashtego remarked;—"Gods and men—both brawlers"; which stands for *blasphemy*.

The Irish sailor, with the traditional Irish love for *strife*, cried;—"The Virgin be blessed, a row! Plunge in with ye!"

But the English sailor, with his native sense of *justice,* insisted upon "Fair play! Snatch the Spaniard's knife! A ring, A ring!"

The old Manx sailor remarked, that in the ring of the horizon, "Cain struck Abel. Sweet work, right work! No," thereby passing *judgement*.

The Mate's voice was then heard, giving orders to reef the sails, which showed *prudence*.

All the sailors immediately scattered to perform their work, upon which their *self-preservation* depended; while poor Pip cringed and cowered under the windlass, the complete embodiment of *fear*.

Objection may be raised to the foregoing interpretation, on the ground that the same process could be applied to any conversation. Well, in fact, it could; for daily dialogue is motivated by various thoughts and emotions. But inasmuch as Melville admitted that "the whole book was susceptible of an allegorical construction," there is nothing gratuitous in assuming any episode in it to be allegorical, if it is susceptible of an interpretation which is consistent with the general subject matter.